THE JOHNS HOPKINS UNIVERSITY STUDIES IN HISTORICAL AND POLITICAL SCIENCE

Under the Direction of the Department of History, Political Economy, and Political Science

SERIES LXXXII
1964

NUMBER 1

A RURAL SOCIETY IN MEDIEVAL FRANCE:
THE GÂTINE OF POITOU IN THE ELEVENTH AND TWELFTH CENTURIES

A RURAL SOCIETY IN MEDIEVAL FRANCE:

The Gâtine of Poitou in the Eleventh and Twelfth Centuries

By

GEORGE T. BEECH

BALTIMORE

THE JOHNS HOPKINS PRESS

1964

Printed in the United States of America
Library of Congress Catalog Card Number 64–16307

This book has been brought to publication with the
assistance of a grant from The Ford Foundation

To my wife:

BEATRICE H. BEECH

PREFACE

I would like to express my gratitude to the founders and administrators of the Gustav Bissing Fund who made possible a year of research in France, and to the administrators of the Faculty Research Fund of Western Michigan University for assistance in this country. M. François Villard, the archivist of the Department of the Vienne, was extraordinarily helpful both in finding documents and in providing criticism; as were also Professor Marcel Garaud of the University of Poitiers, and the directors and members of the Centre d'Études Supérieures de Civilisation Médiévale in Poitiers. But this study would not have been possible without the advice and encouragement of the late Professor Sidney Painter of The Johns Hopkins University and of Professors Fred A. Cazel, Jr., of the University of Connecticut, and Frederic C. Lane of Johns Hopkins.

GEORGE T. BEECH

TABLE OF CONTENTS

A RURAL SOCIETY IN MEDIEVAL FRANCE:

THE GÂTINE OF POITOU IN THE ELEVENTH AND TWELFTH CENTURIES

INTRODUCTION

From many points of view the eleventh and twelfth centuries were the central period in the history of medieval Europe. Coming after the uncertainty of the later Carolingian era it was a time of recovery and advance with the most spectacular change being the reform and consolidation of the medieval church under the papacy. Those same centuries, and perhaps the tenth as well, were also a turning point in other respects, for it was then that Europeans created, out of the ruins of the Carolingian Empire, the political and economic framework for a new society. Movements such as agricultural expansion, growth of population, revival of trade, emergence of feudal institutions, and the rise of feudal monarchies dominated this period as thoroughly in one sense as did religious reformation in another.

This book is a study of the society of a small *pays* (country or region) in western France at that time. Its purpose is to observe at a local level the great movements then sweeping western Europe. Precisely how did the inhabitants of the Gâtine clear and settle their country, what was the nature of the colonization movement, when did feudal and seigneurial institutions spread through the society, and what was the structure of the noble and peasant classes? Did the society of the Gâtine evolve along the same lines as the societies of other parts of France or did it deviate from the general picture? And, if so, why? In attempting to answer some of these questions it is hoped that this regional study will contribute to the understanding of the society of medieval France as a whole.

It is not, however, in the same category as the more ambitious and brilliantly executed studies of scholars like Déléage, Boutruche, Genicot, Perrin, and Duby. The time span covered is shorter, the area smaller, and documentation much poorer. Where the number of separate acts available for other areas runs into the thousands, the Gâtine is able to furnish only some hundreds,

15

and many of these are abbreviated in form. A further drawback, but one shared by all social historians, is the one-sided nature of the sources. All are ecclesiastical, and consequently expose one to the danger of generalizing too freely about lay society on the basis of religious records.

Despite these shortcomings, it is felt that a study of the Gâtine offers the possibility of fruitful results. For one thing it had the advantage of being, as it still is today, a region whose inhabitants had an identity of their own quite distinct from their neighbors. Thus as early as 1039 a nearby monastic chronicler referred to the scattered farmers of the country as *Gastinenses*, or men of the Gâtine. Furthermore, the excellent book by Dr. Louis Merle on agriculture and society in the Gâtine from the sixteenth to the eighteenth centuries illuminates many aspects of the earlier period which otherwise would not have been understood, thereby partially compensating for the gaps in the records for the earlier period. Finally a history of the Gâtine may begin to make restitution for some of the neglect which the medieval province of Poitou has suffered at the hands of social historians.

CHAPTER I

THE COUNTRY, ITS SETTLEMENT AND ITS ECONOMY

The Gâtine of Poitou is a region situated in what was the medieval French province of Poitou and what is now the department of the Deux-Sèvres some 30 miles west of the city of Poitiers.[1] To avoid confusion with several other smaller localities in Poitou which have the same name, it is sometimes referred to as the Gâtine of Parthenay, the capital of the region. Although modern geographers and historians debate about the exact location of its boundaries they agree that in shape it resembles an irregular circle about 35 miles in diameter.[2]

The Gâtine is a country distinguished from the surrounding flatlands on the east and south by an uneven landscape of hills and valleys and by a relatively higher elevation, although in no place does this exceed 876 feet above sea level. Nevertheless, a glance at a relief map reveals a strip of country in shades of brown constrasted with the green of the plain of Poitou to the south and east, and the light green of the bocage of the Vendée on the northwest. The contemporary traveler, upon entering the Gâtine from the south or east, notices a gradual change in the landscape as the flat expanses of the plain give way to a rolling

---

[1] See map No. 1, p. 19.

[2] See map No. 2, p. 33. Robert Bobin, *La Gâtine; étude de géographie* (Niort, 1926), Belisaire Ledain, *La Gâtine historique et monumentale* (2nd ed.; Parthenay, 1897), and Louis Merle, *La métairie et l'évolution agraire de la Gâtine poitevine.* Les hommes et la terre, II, Ecole pratique des hautes études, VI⁰ section, Centre de recherches historiques (Paris, 1948), all have touched on the subject of limits with their differences attributable to their different approaches. Ledain viewed the region as coinciding with the barony of Parthenay, Bobin as a geographical entity, and Merle as a country distinguished from its neighbors by the farming habits and customs of its inhabitants. If exactitude is difficult to attain in the twentieth century, it is out of the question for the twelfth.

17

countryside of many small hills and valleys. Instead of spacious open-field farms he sees a pattern of small fields carefully enclosed and separated from each other by high hedges and surrounding ditches. In, or bordering, nearly every field he also notices scattered patches of woods which are seldom large enough or dense enough to be called forests. He has in fact entered a region typical of the west of France, and elsewhere usually called the *bocage.*

Without some preliminary qualifications, however, it would be imprudent to carry too far the assumption that the Gâtine of today resembles that of the eleventh and twelfth centuries. For in the past seventy-five years an enormous work of deforestation has taken place, thus rendering more land available for cultivation, and changing its appearance considerably.[3] To find out what the Gâtine looked like in the Middle Ages there is no better way than that of examining the etymology of the word itself. One encounters the term frequently in French documents of the period, and indeed it has survived on the map to designate several regions and villages in modern France, the best known of these being perhaps the Gâtinais, south of Paris. The old French word *Gastine* is derived from the Latin *vastus*, meaning deserted or wasted and used as an adjective to describe land it means precisely this— wasteland, or land unfit for inhabitants. Normally it referred to land which was too poor to cultivate, but by extension it came to designate any soil which could not be worked without some pre- liminary improvement.

The Gâtine of Poitou was a region which due mainly to the poverty of its soils could support only a meager population. It is situated on a band of granite which is the termination in Poitou of the Armorican massif of the Breton peninsula. This ancient mountain range now has subsided into a series of low hills and shallow valleys covered for the most part with a thin sandy topsoil. With the aid of fertilizers and careful rotation of crops present day Gâtine farmers manage to harvest rye and buckwheat from this impoverished soil, but to grow better grains, and on a large scale, is impossible now as it was formerly.

Like most of Poitou the Gâtine is subject to a mild, humid climate due to its proximity to the sea and to the fact that pre- vailing winds are from the south and southwest, bringing warmer

---

[3] Bobin, *La Gâtine*, p. 14.

THE GÂTINE IN 12ᵀᴴ-CENTURY FRANCE

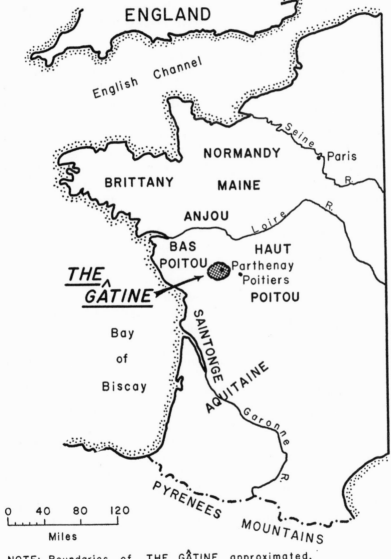

NOTE: Boundaries of THE GÂTINE approximated.

Map 1.

air with them into the north. In addition they blow storm clouds from the Atlantic toward the mainland, depositing heavy rainfall on the Gâtine, the first land barrier of any significant elevation which they meet. The result is a combination of hot, sticky summers and chilly, foggy winters. Add to this the fact that the soil is impermeable to precipitation, thus shedding the rain rather than absorbing it, and one can well imagine that the region was a very wet place indeed.

One of the striking features of the Gâtine today is the extraordinary number of small streams and brooks which seem to trickle through every farm. Taken as a whole these tiny springs form a highly complex water network which never dries up, even in the summer, and which provides an effective drainage system for the region. Two large rivers, the Thouet and the Sèvre-Nantaise, attract most of the brooks which descend from the northeastern slopes of the granite ridge of the Gâtine. Both take their source just west of Secondigny near the commune of le Beugnon with the Sèvre-Nantaise flowing northwest to join the Loire at Nantes. The Thouet links two of the principal towns of the Gâtine, Secondigny and Parthenay, on its course northward before flowing into the Loire at Saumur. Three tributaries of the Sèvre-Niortaise, the Vendée, the Autize, and the Egray absorb most of the water rejected by the southwestern declivity of the Gâtine. For the society of the Middle Ages such an abundant water supply was not without its advantages. Innumerable springs were dammed up to form large ponds, at the outlets of which the mills—so essential to the economy of the Gâtine—could be built. These ponds, which were more common in the Middle Ages than today, were also valued for the fish they yielded.

In the eleventh century the region must have had a forbidding appearance because of its extensive woods and underbrush. Several forests were so large that the authors of charters describing them carefully distinguished them from other smaller woods. Thus a charter of the middle of the twelfth century lists a gift to the monastery of l'Absie of ". . . part of the great woods of les Alleuds as it is marked off with ditches and crosses from the upper path of Vialeria to Prunedaria and the land of Vieillemont."[4] Similar to the forest of Alleuds, which covered a con-

---

[4] ". . . partem magni bosci de alodiis sicuti cum fossis et crucibus signata est a superiori via Vialeriae ad Prunedariam et terram Vellimontis. . . ." *Cartulaires et*

siderable portion of the northwestern Gâtine, were the forest of Brettignolles near le Busseau in the southwest, and the woods of Secondigny and Allonne in the heart of the Gâtine. On the northeastern limit of the region was the forest of Aubigny near Gourgé, while the bois de Magot near St. Martin du Fouilloux and the forêt de la Saisine near Vautebis occupied large areas in the southeast. And no doubt there were others which escaped mention in the documents surviving simply because no one lived in them.[5]

In the Gâtine as in other countries of the *bocage* a lighter kind of woods of stunted oaks and elms, chestnut, and fruit trees existed side by side with the heavier forest.[6] Nearly every charter which describes a parcel of land, no matter how small it might be, mentions an adjoining woods.[7] Designated without much apparent distinction by the terms *nemus, silva,* and *boscum,* this type of woods was usually too small even to have a name.

Just as characteristic of the region as its forests and woods was a dense underbrush which grew in every part of the Gâtine in the eleventh and twelfth centuries. Aside from the numerous general references to hedges, *haiae,* there are few specific allusions to these bushes, but the evidence of place names leaves no doubt that they flourished. That early settlers named farms and hamlets after such growth shows the strong impression it left on their minds.[8] It was this underbrush of thorn bushes, similar to yet taller than heather which, because it proliferated

chartes de l'abbaye de l'Absie (Belisaire Ledain, ed., *Archives historiques du Poitou,* XXV), 91.

[5] For example the forêt du Roux, south of la Ferrière in the eastern Gâtine, which survives today and which in all probability took its name from an eleventh- and twelfth-century family of minor feudal nobility of that region, never appears in contemporary charters.

[6] Place names such as la Châtaigneraie (chestnut), Ulmus (elm), Pomeria (apple), and Quercum (oak) furnish most of the evidence concerning what kind of trees grew in the Gâtine, since direct references are uncommon. Nevertheless, one act of 1218 which deals with the *droits d'usage* in the forêt de la Saisine forbids the cutting down of oak, ash, linden, or beech trees. Alfred Richard (ed.), *Archives du château de la Barre* (St. Maixent, 1868, II), 151.

[7] The following land with woods is only one of many such examples. ". . . Thebaudus Arveus dedit unam masuram terre quae vocatur Calleria, cum bosco et prato. . . ." *Cartulaires de l'Absie,* p. 99.

[8] A few examples are *Audebranderia,* from brandes, and *Broeria* or bruyères, both translated as heather, and *Aubépine* or Hawthorne bush. *Cartulaires de l'Absie,* pp. 19, 49, 51, 67, 71, 76.

rapidly and was extremely difficult to uproot, created the waste-lands, or *terrae gastae*, of the Gâtine.

The combination of woods, undergrowth, poor soil, and damp climate must have made the Gâtine a bleak and uninviting wilder-ness for its early inhabitants. An eloquent witness to this is the monastic biographer of St. Giraud de Salles, founder of the Cistercian abbey of les Châtelliers, on the edge of the Gâtine in 1120, who described the region at that time as ". . . abounding in meadows and woods and streams, and vast solitudes." [9] It was not accidental that the Gâtine attracted monks and nuns of the orders of Citeaux and Fontevrault in great numbers in the twelfth century. The wide-open uninhabited spaces where these religious liked to build their priories and granges, free from secular or worldly attachments, existed in great quantity in the Gâtine.

The Earliest History of the Gâtine

The history of the Gâtine before the eleventh century rests in almost complete obscurity. Only a handful of written documents, none earlier than the middle of the ninth century, survives for the period prior to the year 1000, and archaeological remains are not much more plentiful. Yet this very dearth of evidence strongly suggests sparse settlement before the eleventh century. Bronze axes unearthed at Parthenay, Largeasse, Vasles, and la Ferrière show that human settlements began at least as early as the Celtic period before the Roman occupation of Gaul, and a dolmen found at Faye l'Abbesse pushes the date back into the pre-Celtic period of stone age cultures.[10] Roman occupation of Gaul after the conquests of Julius Caesar stimulated activity in the region. As part of their administrative and defensive policies Roman legionaries in Poitou built a number of roads including two which passed through the southern and western Gâtine crossing at l'Absie: the roads from Angers to Saintes from north to south, and the Chemin des Chaussées running from northeast to south-west between Nantes and Périgueux.[11] The excavation of ruins

[9] ". . . demum quidam intulit Castellaria, utpote pratis et silvis, aquis et fossatis et vastis solitudinibus abundantia . . .," *Acta Sanctorum* (Antwerp and Brussels, 1643 to the present, month *Octobris*, X), 260.

[10] Belisaire Ledain, *Dictionnaire topographique des Deux-Sèvres* (Poitiers, 1902), p. XIII, Introduction.

[11] *Ibid.*, p. XV.

of Roman *villa*'s in three different places in the northeast and
one in the south provides proof of settlement in two other parts
of the region, and the evidence of place names adds to the list.[12]
The survival of names like les Châtelliers, derived from Roman
words for fortifications, in no less than ten places in the Gâtine,
points to an unusual number of military stations in the region,
but this assumption has been verified archaeologically in only
one case.[13] Some twenty other villages and hamlets scattered
through the region whose existence is not attested by written
records until the tenth and eleventh centuries also have names
of Gallo-Roman origin as is indicated by their suffix *iacum*.[14]
Regardless of the exact number, however, a comparison with
other more flourishing provinces of Roman Gaul such as Burgundy
leaves the impression that the Gâtine was still only lightly touched
by human life.[15]

Even less is known about the Gâtine during the period of the
Germanic invasions and the Frankish monarchies than during
the Roman occupation. Aside from a few signs of continued life
in older sites like Gourgé and Parthenay, there is no indication
as to whether the region prospered or declined.[16] To argue that
lack of evidence means retrogression would be unwise since
archaeology may furnish more illumination on this subject in the
future. Only at the end of the Carolingian period in the later
ninth and tenth centuries, at the point where this study begins,
do written documents begin to shed light on life in the Gâtine. At
this time the region was still very sparsely settled, for there is
evidence of the existence of only fourteen communities, all of
which, with one exception, were situated on the richer lands of
the periphery. There were, no doubt, some others which escaped
mention, yet at the same time the relative rarity of references to
the Gâtine in the well documented cartularies of Poitou is striking.

[12] La Raçonnière, Gourgé, and Lamairé in the north and Germond in the south.
Ledain, *La Gâtine*, p. 16.
[13] *Dictionnaire topographique des Deux-Sèvres*, pp. XV, XVI.
[14] Charles Rostaing, *Les noms de Lieux*, Collection " Que sais-je? " (Paris, 1958),
pp. 50, 51, 52. Typical are Partheniacum, Secondiniacum, Jauniacum, etc., which
mean the estates of Parthenius, Secondinius, etc.
[15] André Déléage, *La vie rurale en Bourgogne jusqu'au début du onzième siècle*
(Macon, 1941, I), 103-6.
[16] Tombs reminiscent of Merovingian styles have been found at Gourgé, and a
coin of Charles the Bald has been recovered at Parthenay. Ledain, *La Gâtine*, p. 24.

For instance, the rich cartulary of the nearby abbey of St. Maixent speaks of many sites around its eastern and southern boundaries, but of very few inside its boundaries. The heart of the Gâtine, with its cover of forest and underbrush, appears to have remained untouched except for one village at Allonne.[17]

The nature of these early settlements is very difficult to determine due to the brevity and vagueness of the documents describing them. All are called *villa*'s which suggests that they were related to the large estates of single owners characteristic of Carolingian France. Yet Professor Robert Latouche has shown that in the late Carolingian period the term *villa* also designated other types of settlements including simply any conglomeration of houses, or village, without reference to whether owned by one man or many.[18] Latouche found further that the *régime domaniale*, or *domaine* system, of Carolingian times was rare or nonexistent in much of northwestern France, a country in many respects like the Gâtine.[19] Since vestiges of the *domaine* system were likewise rare in Gâtine in the eleventh and twelfth centuries, it is a distinct possibility that *villa* in the tenth century meant nothing more than a village. In any event it is futile to attempt to learn anything precise about the size of these *villa*'s, and one must be content with the knowledge that they seem to have been self-sustaining agricultural units with their own lands, woods, meadows, vineyards, mills, houses, and sometimes a church.[20]

Even if the Gâtine was sparsely settled to begin with, there are unmistakable signs that in the tenth century its population was declining, and considerable sections of the region were abandoned to return to woods and wasteland. On several occasions new

[17] *Chartularium Sancti Jovini* (Charles Grandmaison, ed., Mémoires de la société de statistique des Deux-Sèvres, XVII), 11, 13. *Chartes et documents pour servir à l'histoire de l'abbaye de St. Maixent* (Alfred Richard, ed., Archives historiques du Poitou, XVI), 81, 89. *Cartulaire de l'abbaye de St. Cyprien de Poitiers* (Louis Redet, ed., Archives historiques du Poitou, III), 89, 91, 108, 112, 325. *Documents pour servir à l'histoire de l'église de Saint Hilaire de Poitiers* (Louis Redet, ed., Mémoires de la société des antiquaires de l'ouest, XIV), 13, 23. Archives d'Indre-et-Loire, Tours, *Abbaye de Bourgueil*, Série H24, No. 3.

[18] Robert Latouche, *The Birth of Western Economy. Economic Aspects of the Dark Ages*, trans. E. M. Wilkinson (New York, 1961), pp. 194–98.

[19] *Ibid.*, pp. 279–80.

[20] All are described in approximately the same language as follows: ". . . in villa que dicitur Valerius, cum domibus, curtiferis, terris, pratis, aquis, aquarumve decursibus, cultum et incultum, quesitum et adinquirendum," *Chartes de St. Maixent*, I, 89.

settlers of the eleventh and twelfth centuries were confronted by
the ruins of once inhabited places such as the remains of the church
of l'Absie found by a hermit around 1100, and the church of
Boismé, which had collapsed around 1040 because of old age
and, presumably, neglect.[21] Destruction of the original settlement
may also explain why the inhabitants of Parthenay, la Peyratte,
Verruyes, and les Châtelliers in the eastern Gâtine established
new villages in the eleventh and twelfth centuries.[22] It is a curious
fact, moreover, that the *vicaria*, a territorial subdivision of the
Carolingian Empire which survived into the tenth and eleventh
centuries, is extremely rare in all of Bas-Poitou from the Gâtine
westward to the ocean. One finds allusions to *vicariae* on the
extreme northern, eastern, and southern edges of the Gâtine,
but none in the heart of the region itself.[23] Such districts may
have ceased to exist simply because most people had fled the
region. Whatever the explanation, and repeated Viking raids
are the most plausible, it is certain that the society of the Gâtine,
never very large, had been severely shaken at the beginning of
the feudal period in French history.[24]

The early eleventh century was a great turning point in the
history of the Gâtine. After a period of uncertainty, when fear
and destruction caused some of its inhabitants to flee, came a
time of colonization and expansion which dwarfed in importance
all other contemporary events. Beginning slowly and sporadically,
it gained its greatest momentum at the end of the eleventh, and
early twelfth centuries when it was sponsored by both the church
and the nobility, and then gradually subsided at the end of the
twelfth century. By comparison with adjoining regions colonization never produced a sudden or spectacular increase in the number

[21] ". . . Petrus de Bunt heremita in territorio Gastinae, in loco qui dicitur Absia,
materias dirutas veteris ecclesiae reperit . . ." *Cartulaires de l'Absie*, p. 7.
". . . ecclesias de Bomniaco, unam in honore Sancti Petri antiqua vetustate diru-
tam. . . ." *Cartulaire de St. Cyprien*, p. 106.
[22] Each of these places was located near the old settlement which seems to have
been uninhabited as, for example, Vieux Verruyes. *Chartes de St. Maixent*, I, 231.
Cartulaire de l'abbaye de Talmond (Louis de la Boutetière, ed., Mémoires de la
société des antiquaires de l'ouest, XXXVI). *Cartulaire de la l'abbaye royale de
Notre-Dame des Châtelliers* (Louis Duval, ed., Mémoires de la société de statistique
des Deux-Sèvres, 1872), p. 9. Jean Besly, *Histoire des comtes de Poictou et des
ducs de Guyenne, contenant ce qui s'est passé de plus mémorable en France depuis
l'an 811 jusques au Roy Louis le Jeune* (Paris, 1647), p. 396.
[23] See below, pp. 43–44.
[24] See below, p. 43.

of inhabitants, nor did it result in a dense population. Nevertheless, the foundations of Gâtine society had been so thoroughly laid
that by the end of the twelfth century a map of the region is
fully recognizable beside one of the present day.

Colonization took place in two phases more or less distinct
from one another both in time and in the areas affected. During
the eleventh century settlers preferred to settle in communities
which were already established rather than to found new villages
in virgin country. Almost all of the settlements of this period
had place names of an earlier origin, and included among their
number were the fourteen villages known to have been occupied
in the ninth and tenth centuries. Once again it is difficult to
determine the character of these settlements because of the terse
descriptions of contemporaries who usually called them *villa*'s or
parrochia's (parish), but who also often wrote nothing but their
place names. However, the gradual replacement of *villa* by *parrochia* after about 1060, and the fact that all these places had
churches demonstrates that they were hamlets or small villages
which were centers for the religious life of the countryside.[25]
Religious expansion was indeed one of the principal manifestations
of agricultural and population expansion in the Gâtine in the
eleventh and twelfth centuries. At least one-third and perhaps
more of the tenth-century *villa*'s had churches, and the parish
system itself doubtless goes back to the late Roman Empire and
early Middle Ages, but the period of greatest church building
was immediately after the year 1000.[26] Only in a few cases do
records yield the actual date of construction, but architectural and
stylistic features prove that at least thirty-three or almost one-
half the stone edifices in the Gâtine today date entirely or in part
from the eleventh and twelfth centuries.[27]

The expansion of older settlements found its most characteristic
expression in the building of burgs. Between 1040 and 1100
records attest the founding of thirteen burgs throughout the

[25] Emile Amann and Auguste Dumas, *L'église au pouvoir des laiques* (888–1057).
L'histoire de l'église depuis les origines jusqu'à nos jours, VII. (Paris, 1948),
265–66.

[26] Pierre Imbart de la Tour, *Les origines religieuses de la France; les paroisses
rurales du IVe au XIe siècle* (Paris, 1900), pp. 347–48.

[27] René Crozet, *L'Art Roman en Poitou* (Paris, 1948), pp. 13, 14, 34, 38, 40, 65,
76–78, 101, 102, 106, 107, 116, 119, 124, 126, 127, 130, 134, 136, 138, 139, 144,
150, 152, 159, 164, 176, 182, 183, 185, 198, 206, 213, 227, 231, 270, 271.

region, and there were certainly more for which no evidence survives.[28] Since detailed charters commemorating the foundation of several of them are still extant, there is more information about this phase of colonization than any other. The burg was identical to other rural communities except that its inhabitants enjoyed an exemption from certain sales taxes and seigneurial dues paid by all other peasants. In appearance it consisted primarily of the houses which the burgers built in a cluster around the village church.[29] In one case the burg of la Peyratte was situated within the cemetery of the parish church, " et burgum intra cimiterium." This rather unusual location is explained by the fact that there it enjoyed the immunity of a sacred place.[30] Just like other communities, most burgs contained a mill and an oven where their inhabitants might mill their grain and bake their bread, and in all likelihood most had wine presses.[31] It was usually specified by the seigneur donating the burg that the burgers would have a market in front of the church for buying and selling their goods.[32]

To distinguish them from adjoining lands under other jurisdictions, some sort of small barrier was erected around the limits of each burg. The monks of St. Paul of Parthenay were allowed to use the woods of the lord of Parthenay for enclosing their

[28] See map No. 2, p. 33. The references to each of these burgs are as follows: Allonne, Archives de la Haute-Loire, le Puy, *Abbaye de la Chaise-Dieu*, H185, Nos. 2 and 3. Chiché, *Chartularium Sancti Jovini*, pp. 23–24. St. Paul and St. Jean of Parthenay and la Ferrière, *Cartulaire de Cormery, précédé de l'histoire de l'abbaye et de la ville de Cormery* (J. Bourasse, ed., Mémoires de la société archéologique de Touraine, 1861), pp. 90–93. La Peyratte, *Cartulaire de Talmond*, p. 78. Pugny, *Chartes de l'Abbaye de Nouaillé* (Dom Pierre de Monsabert, ed., Archives historiques du Poitou, XLIX), 228–29. Secondigny, Bibliothèque Nationale, Paris, Collection Gaignières, *Abbaye de Bourgueil*, Fonds Latin 17127, p. 379. Saint Lin, *Chartes de St. Maixent*, I, 120. Parthenay-le-Vieux, J. Besly, *Histoire des comtes*, p. 396. Gourgé, *Extrait du Cartulaire de l'abbaye de Bourgueil* (private copy of M. J. Goupil de Bouillé of Pavée, Bourgueil, Indre-et-Loire), p. 139. Boismé, *Cartulaire de St. Cyprien*, p. 106. Breuil Bernard, *Cartulaire de St. Cyprien*, p. 112.

[29] ". . . omnes qui circa ecclesiam noviter edificatam domos suas construxerint . . .," Bibliothèque Nationale, Gaignières, F. L. 17127, p. 379.

[30] *Cartulaire de Talmond*, p. 78. On the immunity of a cemetery, see Latouche, *The Birth of Western Economy*, p. 279.

[31] *Cartulaire de Nouaillé*, pp. 228–29. *Cartulaires de l'Absie*, pp. 2, 81. Bibliothèque Nationale, Gaignières, F. L. 17127, p. 379. *Cartulaire de Cormery*, pp. 90–93. Bibliothèque Nationale, N. A. 2414, No. 789. Besly, *Histoire*, p. 396.

[32] ". . . licentiamque vendendi et emendi non solum panes sed etiam alias res. . ." Bibliothèque Nationale, Gaignières, F. L. 17127, p. 379.

burg and their fields.[33] No exact descriptions survive to tell whether this enclosure was a hedge or some kind of small fence, but in any event it did not serve military or defensive purposes as is shown by the burgs location outside the castle walls. And, in fact, whenever a burg was erected at a place dominated by a fortification it was outside the walls, ". . . apud Secundiniacum foris castrum. . . ."[34] Thus in one very important respect the burgs of the Gâtine bore no resemblance to the fortified burgs of medieval Germany. Beyond this enclosure lay the land which the burgers cleared and planted with grains and grapevines.

The building of burgs was an organized undertaking and not ► a matter of individual initiative. Responsibility for the task and credit for the accomplishment belongs to the nobility and regular clergy. Nobles in every case provided the land for the burg, relinquished their patronage over its church, and exempted its inhabitants from some of the exactions customarily levied on peasants.[35] On the other hand monks from several great Benedictine monasteries of Poitou such as St. Cyprien of Poitiers, St. Pierre of Bourgueil, and St. Maixent of the town of the same name usually supervised the construction of the burg and invariably administered it once it was occupied.

The ability to attract settlers was essential to the success of the proposed burg. A remarkable charter of the lords of Parthenay, Ebbo and Gelduin, issued in 1092 when they established the burg of Parthenay-le-Vieux, illustrates that their solution to this problem was to offer the prospective settler immunity to the sales and road taxes normally collected from people going to market. In other words burgers, while still subject to all other taxes on peasants, would have the prospect of retaining some of the profit on the goods they sold. In addition they asserted that anyone not subject to their authority, no matter who his lord or what his origin, might come and live peacefully in the burg without external disturbance.[36] Thus they not only welcomed persons

---

[33] ". . . licentiam de silvis suis faciendi . . . ad clausuram burgi et agrorum. . . ." *Cartulaire de Cormery*, pp. 90–93.

[34] *Ibid.*, Bibliothèque Nationale, Gaignières, F. L. 17127, p. 379. Besly, *Histoire*, p. 396.

[35] Of the twelve burgs for which the donor is known, three were founded by lesser nobility and nine by castellans or men from the upper ranks of that class such as the lords of Parthenay, Verruyes, Bressuire, and Talmond.

[36] Text given below, p. 122, footnote 76.

living on land entirely removed from their control, or in effect
people from outside the Gâtine, but also guaranteed them protection against the possibility that their former lords might attempt
to force them to return to their original tenures. Whatever the
benefits they received, the fact that newly arriving peasants were
treated as *hospites*, in French *hôtes* and meaning settlers, shows
that it was they who did the manual labor of building houses,
clearing land and cultivating it.[37]

The eleventh century was also the great period of castle
building in the Gâtine. As an aristocracy arose from the new
population, the most powerful of its members constructed castles
to consolidate more firmly their position. In all likelihood these
military structures were added to already inhabited sites, but the
evidence of archaeology and place names can corroborate this in
only three of the seven castles; Parthenay, Secondigny, and Germond. Leaving for a later context a discussion of the circumstances surrounding their construction, it will suffice here to note
that the lords of Parthenay had established control over all of
them by the end of the eleventh century.

Without abating in the least, the colonization of the Gâtine
nonetheless gradually changed its character around the end of
the eleventh century. Instead of establishing themselves in or at
the edge of older villages, settlers increasingly struck out into
the wilder, uninhabited countryside to locate their farms. But
since these settlements were possible only after trees and bushes
were cut down and the land cleared for cultivation, a concerted
movement of deforestation preceded and accompanied this phase
of colonization. Monastic settlements then made small but ever
increasing inroads on the large forests of the Gâtine, including
the woods of les Alleux in the west, the bois de Magot in the east,
and the fôret de Secondigny and bois d'Allonne in the central
part of the region.[38] And everywhere, what had once been

---

[37] ". . . Concessit etiam ut si aliquid in burgo Parthenaci non habens proprium
domum voluerit transire in burgum St. Pauli et illic domum facere, non prohibeatur
ibidem facere *hospitari* . . .,"*Cartulaire de Cormery*, pp. 90–93. The term *hospes* was
commonly used to describe colonizers in medieval France. Latouche, *The Birth of
Western Economy*, p. 281.

[38] *Cartulaires de l'Absie*, pp. 79, 80, 91, 135. *Cartulaire de St. Cyprien*, p. 280.
Bibliothèque de la ville de Poitiers, *Dom Fonteneau: Les mémoires ou le recueil de
diplômes, chartes, notices et autres actes authentiques pour servir à l'histoire du
Poitou, accompagnés de notes critiques, historiques, etc.,* I, 391–99. Archives de la
Vienne, Poitiers, *Abbaye de Fontaine-le-comte,* Série H, carton 6, liasse 10, No. 7.

unrelieved woodland, heather, and underbrush now yielded to an occasional clearing of fields, meadows, and houses. Very few charters speak directly of the actual labor of deforestation, but there is abundant indirect evidence of it.[39] Woods surrounded or bordered part of virtually every exploitation mentioned in the twelfth century as a vivid reminder of how much remained to be done.[40] The peasant was sometime called, quite specifically, a colonizer, *hospes*, and his dwelling, a newly constructed shelter, *arbergamentum*.[41]

The high incidence of *terrage* and *complant*, taxes proportional to the harvest in grain and grapes, and elsewhere in France found in newly cleared areas, also points to recent colonization in many parts of the Gâtine.[42] To be sure the rewards were not always commensurate with the labor involved, for several landlords in Lamairé who had just planted vineyards anticipated, probably on the basis of past experience, the possibility of failure.[43] Yet continuing their work in full force throughout most of the twelfth century, by 1200 the new settlers had succeeded in sprinkling the empty gaps in the Gâtine with a multitude of tiny agricultural exploitations, many of which have the same names and same isolated character still today.

Two different groups of men stimulated and carried out this phase of colonization. Of great consequence was the work of the monks of Citeaux and Fontevrault. As a result of enthusiasm for the monastic reform movement of Citeaux then sweeping western Europe, two monasteries following the rule of that order

---

[39] Exceptions include the references to clearings at Brettignoles and in the bois de Magot. ". . . ut habeant licentiam inibi excolendi, edificandi, plantandi, construendi . . .," Bibliothèque Nationale, Gaignières, F. L. 17127, pp. 127–28. ". . . decimam totam de silva Maingodi que noviter excolitur. . . ." *Cartulaire de St. Cyprien*, p. 280.

[40] See above, p. 21, footnote 7.

[41] *Cartulaire de St. Cyprien*, p. 113. Archives de Maine-et-Loire, Angers, *Pancarta et Cartularium Fontis Ebraudi*, Série 101H225, No. 35. The following passage from an act of 1267 illustrates the meaning of *arbergamentum*, or its verb *arbergare*. ". . . et virgule sito inter dictos domos, poterunt arbergare unum hominem. . . ." MSS Dom Fonteneau, I, 391–99.

[42] *Cartulaires de l'Absie*, pp. 1, 79, 85, 92, 105, 107, 109, etc. *Cartulaire de Talmond*, pp. 164, 68, 70. *Chartularium Sancti Jovini*, p. 24, etc. Georges Dubq, *L'économie rurale et la vie des campagnes dans l'occident médiéval (France, Angleterre, Empire, XIe–XVe siècles). Essai de synthèse et perspectives de recherches.* Collection historique. (Paris, 1962, II), 442.

[43] See below, p. 104.

were organized in the Gâtine in 1120, one at l'Absie in the west and the other at les Châtelliers on the southeastern boundary of the region.[44] Since its rule demanded freedom from secular obligations and complete detachment from the outside world, the Cistercian Order was particularly well suited to barren, thinly populated regions like the Gâtine. During the remainder of the twelfth century the monastery of l'Absie proceeded to build up a network of at least six priories, or small religious houses, scattered in uninhabited spots throughout the entire northern part of the region. It also owned a good many granges in the western Gâtine which lacked priories and were farmed for it exclusively by laymen.[45]

An equally significant contribution to the settlement of the Gâtine was made by the monastery of Fontevrault located thirty miles to the north near the Loire River. Created in 1096 by an ascetic, Robert d'Arbrissel, the monastery of Fontevrault belongs to the same movement which gave birth to the Cistercian Order. Seeking the solitude they thought conducive to a purer contemplation, the nuns and monks of Fontevrault were soon drawn to the Gâtine in imposing numbers. At the end of the twelfth century priories or granges belonging to that monastery had been founded in no less than seven different places in the Gâtine, and lands or rights acquired in numerous others.[46]

Whereas, for religious reasons the monks of l'Absie and Fontevrault may have colonized uninhabited regions more systematically than others, it is nonetheless clear that from the end of the eleventh century on there was a similar movement on the part of secular society in the Gâtine. A veritable flood of new place names of recent French origin, scattered through the interior of

[44] *Cartulaires de l'Absie*, p. 8. " Chronicon Sancti-Maxentii Pictavensis," *Chroniques des églises d'Anjou*, Paul Marchegay and Emile Mabille, eds. Société de l'histoire de France (Paris, 1869), p. 429.

[45] See map No. 2, p. 33. *Cartulaires de l'Absie*, pp. 10, 27, 79, 92, 109, 132. It is possible that some of these *domaines* were among the anonymous granges located in the lands of the lord of Parthenay in 1169. ". . . et grangiarum eius quae sunt in terra mea . . .," *ibid.*, p. 81.

[46] Priories included la Poraire, Billy, Lorge Boisseau, Taçonnerie, la Gondoinière, Montibeuf, and Monbertin. See map No. 2, p. 33. Bibliothèque Nationale, Paris, *Pancarta et Cartularium Fontis Ebraudi*, Nouvelles Acquisitions 2414, No. 789. Archives de Maine-et-Loire, Angers, *L'abbaye de Fontevrault; extraits des cartulaires, chartes, obituaires, régistres*, Série 101H225 bis, Nos. 41, 124, 167, 330, 396, Archives de Maine-et-Loire, Angers, Fonds de Fontevrault, Série 231H1, No. 3.

the region, testifies to this development. Contrasted with the Gallo-Roman names of the eleventh century villages, almost all of these were composed of the name of a person followed by the suffix *eria* which in the twelfth century was a common way of referring to the land and dwelling of the man who cleared and cultivated it or simply the man then living on it.[47] For instance *Berauderia*, today the farm of la Braudière near Secondigny, was land opened to farming by one Beraudus. The peasant who was working that land around 1130, Giraud Beraud, had either cleared it and named it after himself, or else he had taken its name, perhaps as the descendant of an earlier Beraud.[48]

These settlements, most of which had individual place names, were either isolated or at least some distance removed from other inhabited places. Their names, *borderia* and manse, indicate that they were farms for one or two, or perhaps more families, but not entire communities. Yet, small as they may have been, both the manse and the *borderia* were self-contained agricultural units comprising woods, meadows for pasture, the various fields under cultivation, houses for the inhabitants, and sometimes even a mill.[49]

By the end of the twelfth century the pattern of settlement of the Gâtine had been definitively established. Colonization continued after that time but at a much slower pace than before and in no way changing the character of the region. Approximately two hundred years of sustained effort had populated the region with a series of settlements varying from a handful of castles to some sixty-five villages, each built around a parish church, and to a mass of tiny separate farms. Dispersion of population was easily the outstanding feature of society of the Gâtine for, with the exception of Parthenay, towns were non-existent. Parthenay itself had grown by leaps and bounds to strengthen its position as undisputed political and commercial capital of the region. By the end of the century no less than seven parish churches had been built there, and in 1202 the castle walls were extended to enclose a much larger section of the town

---

[47] Rostaing, *Les noms de Lieux*, p. 91.

[48] *Cartulaires de l'Absie*, p. 10.

[49] The following is a description of a typical twelfth century *borderie*; " Rainaldus Boins concessit monachis Sancti Cypriani in Bomniaco terram de Brollio, cultam et incultam, borderiatam totam una cum silva et arbergamentis, pratis ex duabus partibus cum rivulis foncium determinantibus." *Cartulaire de St. Cyprien*, p. 113.

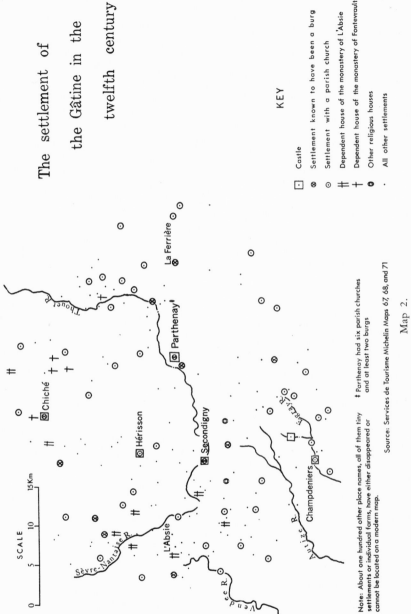

The settlement of
the Gâtine in the
twelfth century

KEY

☐ Castle

⊗ Settlement known to have been a burg

⊙ Settlement with a parish church

‡ Dependent house of the monastery of L'Absie

† Dependent house of the monastery of Fontevrault

⊕ Other religious houses

· All other settlements

Note: About one hundred other place names, all of them tiny settlements or individual farms, have either disappeared or cannot be located on a modern map.

‡ Parthenay had six parish churches and at least two burgs

Source: Services de Tourisme Michelin Maps 67, 68, and 71

Map 2.

SCALE
0   5   10   15 Km

Thouet R.

Sèvre-Nantaise R.

Vendée R.

Autize R.

Égray R.

Chiché

Hérisson

L'Absie

Parthenay

Secondigny

La Ferrière

Champdeniers

than had been originally fortified.[50] But other than Parthenay not a single place in the Gâtine was large enough to warrant more than one parish church. Not even those sites like Secondigny, Champdeniers, or Ternant, which boasted a castle and consequently some military importance, ever succeeded in attracting inhabitants in the same degree as did Parthenay. Statistics on the population are totally impossible to obtain in view of the evidence available, but a lack of towns and a dispersed population, of course, also meant a sparse population for the entire region.

Agricultural expansion in the eleventh and twelfth centuries was not unique to the Gâtine, but a regional manifestation of a phenomenon common to most parts of France and western Europe at that time. Consequently it is not surprising that it occurred in much the same way and for many of the same reasons as elsewhere in France.[51] The establishment of the noble family of Parthenay as the supreme power in the region created conditions of relatively greater peace and stability than in the tenth century, despite periodic feudal wars. Peasants in considerable numbers were available and looking for new land, being willing to accept even the poorer soils of the Gâtine, although it is impossible to determine whether they were mainly outsiders or the offspring of larger families within the region who were experiencing a land shortage. The hope of profiting from the European-wide revival of commerce unquestionably stimulated some of the nobility, and especially the lords of Parthenay, to found burgs, even though most of these became merely agricultural settlements.[52] And one cannot discount the fact that any new land under cultivation brought new revenues to its landlord. The current of reform moving through the European monasteries in the twelfth century also inspired ambitious and industrious monks to participate in the movement of expansion in the Gâtine. All of these factors contributed materially to the settlement of the region which, in the final analysis, with its thin, widely scattered population, was less complete than in other parts of France. Yet in precisely these

---

[50] Ledain, *La Gâtine*, p. 81.

[51] General treatments of this subject may be found in G. Duby, *L'économie rurale,* I, 131–261; and Richard Koebner, " The Settlement and Colonisation of Europe," *Cambridge Economic History of Europe from the Decline of the Roman Empire. The Agrarian Life of the Middle Ages* (Cambridge, 1941, I), 1–88.

[52] The exemption for burgers from road and sales taxes when carrying goods to and from market makes this clear. *Cartulaire de Cormery*, pp. 90–93.

characteristics the Gâtine resembles, in a striking fashion, several other regions in southern and northern medieval France, but above all the western part of the country where the *bocage* often predominated.[53] The explanation for this settlement pattern is surely to be traced back to the poverty of the soil which could support only a limited number of people in any given area, and which therefore must have encouraged men to spread out over the countryside rather than to congregate.

The Economy of the Gâtine

Farming provided the economic foundation for life in the Gâtine in this period, and its basic elements were the peasant farm and the *seigneurie*. The latter was the unit formed by the domain, or land reserved for the *seigneur*, and the peasant tenures held from him. For the Gâtine belonged very largely to nobility from whom peasants, with very few allods or freeholds of their own, rented most of their land. Ecclesiastical and lay nobility divided the region among themselves, but the records do not permit even a guess as to the percentage of the total held by either. Ecclesiastical *seigneuries*, of which we have a much better record because all surviving sources are religious, reached into every corner of the region from the burgs into isolated rural areas. The monks of l'Absie, Fontevrault, Bourgueil, and St. Maixent owned the most extensive land, but a half-dozen other houses held estates there including such famous ones as Cormery in the Touraine, la Chaise-Dieu (Haute-Loire), and Cluny in Burgundy. Moreover the acts of donation filling the cartularies of those monasteries reveal that their *seigneuries* grew steadily in size during this period.

Very little is known about the structure of the *seigneurie* in the Gâtine, such as, for instance, the relative size of the domain and the peasant tenures. Yet a later discussion will show that peasants had relatively few obligations to their landlords whose economic control over them was slight. However, over and above

---

[53] G. Duby, *L'économie rurale*, I, 161–65; R. Latouche, *The Birth of Western Economy*, pp. 279–80; Charles Higounet, "Observations sur la seigneurie rurale et l'habitat en Rouergue du IXᵉ au XIVᵉ siècle," *Annales du Midi* (1950), pp. 121–34; A. Chédeville, "Étude de la mise en valeur et du peuplement du Maine au XIᵉ siècle d'après les documents de l'abbaye de St. Vincent du Mans," *Annales de Bretagne* (1960), pp. 208–25.

this another form of *seigneurie*, the territorial *seigneurie*, which was imposed in the eleventh and twelfth centuries, came to subjugate peasants to another set of lords, mainly the castellans of the region, and added substantially to their economic burdens.

During the later tenth and eleventh centuries, the manse, *mansus*, *mansura*, and *masura*, was the amount of land considered sufficient for a single peasant household and is the only kind of exploitation to be encountered. However as the population of the Gâtine increased toward the end of the eleventh century, the *borderia*, or one-half a manse, replaced it as the commonest type of peasant tenure. The division of the manse into smaller agricultural units occasionally proceeded even further until there were some peasant farms of one-quarter of the original size, or the *quarteria*, but on the whole the *borderia* was most prevalent.

Contemporaries never gave the exact size of either of these exploitations, but according to the *Vieux coustumier de Poictou* of the fifteenth century, a *borderia* was the amount of land which could be plowed yearly by a team of two oxen and a manse the amount of land which could be plowed yearly by one of four oxen. In the sixteenth century *borderia*'s in the Gâtine ranged in size from two to fifteen *hectares*, or from five to thirty-seven acres, a variation presumably due to the differing productivity of the soil, and there is no good reason for believing that either the *borderia* or the manse had changed essentially between the twelfth and the sixteenth centuries.[54]

In appearance most peasant exploitations probably resembled the *borderia* of le Breuil in the parish of Boismé. When Rainald Boins gave that land to the abbey of St. Cyprien around 1120, he described it as including houses, a woods, two meadows divided by streams, and both cultivated and waste land.[55] Woods were absolutely essential to peasant life at that time and a small patch seems to have made up at least a part of every *borderia* or manse. It was invaluable as a source of building material for houses, mills, and other facilities, and dead and fallen trees

---

[54] Merle, *La métairie*, p. 73.

[55] " Rainaldus Boins concessit monachis Sancti Cypriani in Bomniaco terram de Brollio, cultam et incultam, borderiatam totam una cum silva et arbergamentis, pratis ex duabus partibus cum rivulis foncium determinantibus." *Cartulaire de St. Cyprien*, p. 113.

supplied firewood. There is also evidence that the larger forest areas in the Gâtine were prized for their beehives which yielded the only sweetening substance available at that time.[56]

The remaining land on the *borderia* was divided into three parts, one section under cultivation, another of wasteland, and the third, a meadow. It is interesting to note that in the only two cases where specifications were given, meadows were called *quarteria*, that is they equaled one-quarter of a manse in area.[57] Even though it is impossible to confirm that this was always the ratio between fields and meadow, it is nevertheless remarkable that farms of the seventeenth century contained precisely those percentages of both kinds of land.[58] Lying mainly along streams, these meadows furnished hay, *faenum*, for the livestock and served as pasture after cutting. Farmers also grazed animals on their fields between harvest time and the next planting. The peasants of the Gâtine kept cattle, pigs, sheep, and occasionally goats, but that should not lead one to believe that raising of livestock was as vital to rural economy as agriculture.[59] The sheep clearly contributed wool to the woolen industry in Parthenay, but in the sixteenth and seventeenth centuries farmers needed large tracts of meadowland just to maintain the oxen used as draught animals and did not attempt to raise beef or produce dairy products for the market.[60] It can hardly have been different in the twelfth century.

The rest of the *borderia* consisted of arable fields and waste land, *terra culta et inculta*. For the seventeenth century Dr. Merle found that anywhere from 6 to 28 per cent of the land of the *métairie* was waste land and never plowed, whereas from 40 to 60 per cent could be used for crops.[61] At any given time, however, only one-third of the arable was planted, the other two-thirds, according to the *Vieux coustumier*, being divided between the land

---

[56] ". . . de reliquis boscis de Alodiis quicquid praedicti monachi et homines sui capere vellent ad omne opus abbatiae et omnium grangiarum suarum et examina apum quae ipsi et homines sui in ipsis boscis invenire possent. . . ." *Cartulaires de l'Absie*, p. 91.

[57] *Ibid.*, pp. 22, 30.

[58] Merle, *La métairie*, p. 107.

[59] " Tebaudus Aans faenum rastrorum et faenum scissionis mullonum (dedit). . . ." *Cartulaires de l'Absie*, p. 108. ". . . Willelmus Chabot concessit decimam . . . bestiarum, lanarum, cherveorium. . . ." *Ibid.*, p. 94.

[60] Merle, *La métairie*, p. 146.

[61] *Ibid.*, p. 107.

left fallow and used for grazing, and land which was plowed but not planted. The peasant thus cultivated each field, at the most, only once every three years. The sources for the twelfth century are silent on this subject but it stands to reason that the agriculture of the medieval period can scarcely have been more efficient than that of the later period. The fact remains that owing to the poor soil and excessive precipitation, agriculture was a difficult and marginal venture in the medieval Gâtine, and only rye could be grown there with any consistent success. Wheat was quite out of the question except at two isolated spots in the region, Lamairé and Pugny, and oats were in evidence in only one or two places in the southwestern Gâtine.[62] Nevertheless, the large number of mills which ecclesiastical records bring to light in this period is convincing proof of the importance of grain crops in the economy of the time. Of course locating and building mills was no problem in the Gâtine where running water was plentifully available. The monastery of l'Absie alone owned fully or in part at least fourteen mills in the region, and it was just one among many rich land-owners. The abundant waterways of the region were of economic value in another way. In many instances brooks were dammed up to form the large ponds, so characteristic of the medieval Gâtine, which were greatly valued for fishing.[63] The more important ponds and rivers were the exclusive property of the nobility and particularly the lord of Parthenay, but it is conceivable that peasants had the right of fishing the diminutive brooks which flowed through their farms, and in so doing could sometimes add a delicacy to their dour diets.[64]

It is somewhat difficult to imagine how grapevines, which require a dry soil and moderate rainfall, and which are non-existent there today, could have been grown in the twelfth century. Yet surprisingly enough viticulture was so widespread at that time that many laymen, and not just the secular and regular clergy, set aside a bit of their lands for vines. To be sure it must

[62] References to wheat; *Cartulaires de l'Absie*, pp. 77, 95; to oats, *ibid.*, p. 92. Bibliothèque de Tours, Collection Salmon, MS 1338, p. 264; MS 1339, p. 30.

[63] Even though a number of these large ponds or small lakes are still to be seen in the Gâtine, Dr. Merle reveals that many more were drained in the sixteenth and seventeenth centuries. Merle, *La métairie*, p. 78.

[64] On the monopoly of fishing rights by the lord of Parthenay see, Archives de Haute-Loire, Série 1H185, Nos. 2 and 3. *Cartulaire de Cormery*, pp. 90–93. Bibliothèque Nationale, Gaignières, F. L. 17127, p. 379.

have been undertaken often on an experimental basis, for several individuals who had just begun to plant vines in the parishes of Lamairé and la Peyratte anticipated the possibility of failure.[65] The only way to account for the persistence of men at that time is to agree with M. Latouche that the wine produced must have been of a dreadful quality, but that it was still preferable to none at all.[66]

Most peasants presumably had a small enclosed garden, *olca*, located near their houses, as did the priest of Lamairé.[67] In addition to vegetables both flax and hemp were widely grown for the textile fibers and rope material which they yielded.[68] The chickens which peasants of Pelouaille paid as rent for their land point to the poultry which many farmers doubtless kept.[69]

Economic historians have classified French agriculture into three basic types or *régimes agraires*, each based on a specific kind of field system and farming practices.[70] These were the stripshaped open field, the irregular-shaped open field, and the enclosed field systems. Although the Gâtine falls into the *bocage* area of western France which is normally assigned to the system of enclosed fields, some debate exists as to whether it had that character in the Middle Ages. His research on the *métairie* of the sixteenth through the eighteenth centuries has led Dr. Merle to conclude that the Gâtine in the earlier period must have been a region of irregular-shaped open fields, each continuous with the other, and one where the *vaine pâture*, or collective use of harvested fields for grazing, was practiced by the entire community. Only in the sixteenth century and later did nobility begin to build hedges and enclose fields as part of a sustained effort to regroup their lands and separate them from those of others.[71]

Small fields, varying in area from a few *sextariata*, of about two and one-half acres each, to a single *minata*, or slightly more than one acre, did exist in some quantity in the Gâtine of the

[65] See below, p. 104.
[66] Latouche, *Les origines de l'économie occidentale* (Paris, 1956), p. 322.
[67] *Cartulaire de Talmond*, p. 164.
[68] ". . . Item concesserunt . . . et medietate decime totius ville (Breuil Bernard) de agnis, de lana, de lino, de canaba . . .." *Cartulaire de St. Cyprien*, p. 112. *Canaba* was hemp and *linum* flax.
[69] *Cartulaires de l'Absie*, p. 110.
[70] Marc Bloch, *Les caractères originaux de l'histoire rurale française* (new edition, Paris, 1955, I), 35–65.
[71] Merle, *La métairie*, pp. 76, 77, 83–87, 136.

eleventh and twelfth centuries. Nonetheless men of that era referred several times quite specifically to hedges and ditches enclosing both vineyards and cultivated fields, and one of them leaves the strong impression that they were quite common.[72] In 1162 a dispute over the limits within which the seigneurial agent, the *mestivier,* could collect his lord's revenues, was taken to Peter, bishop of Poitiers. Peter recommended that ". . . all hedges and other things used as barriers . . ." in the *seigneurie* of Vernoux should, along with the mounds on which they stood and the ditches on either side of them be equal in size to those of the *seigneurie* of l'Absie.[73] The manner in which this difference was settled is significant. Only if hedges were the rule rather than the exception would first an episcopal then a seigneurial decree have been necessary to insure that their dimensions were uniform in two different *seigneuries.*

An abundance of small parcels of land and of hedges; this is a contradiction only if one assumes that the Gâtine had a uniform rural character at that time. On the contrary much evidence points to a combination of two different *régimes agraires.* Around the older villages of the region, those settled since Roman times or the early Middle Ages, the existence of a pattern of closely grouped fields, such as those Dr. Merle found in later times, is clearly discernible. For example the donations of Giraud Tolard to the abbot of Talmond are as follows: two and one-half *sextarias* of land *sub Viridario,* seven *sextarias ad Plantas,* and four *sextarias* in another place, but all in the parish of la Peyratte.[74] These were plainly plots of land scattered about in three of the *quartiers,* which were subdivisions, each with its own name, of the *terroir* or land belonging to the inhabitants of the village. Settlements

---

[72] *Cartulaire de Cormery,* pp. 90–93. Besly, *Histoire,* p. 396. *Cartulaire de St. Cyprien,* p. 108. *Cartulaires de l'Absie,* pp. 18, 78, 91. MSS Dom Fonteneau, 1, 391. *Acta Sanctorum,* Octobris, X (Life of Giraud de Salles), p. 260.

[73] ". . . Ex judicio Petri Pictavensis matris ecclesiae, concesserunt infra haiam metive jura. Has iidem Willelmus de Vernol et Gaufridus, consensu et consilio tam suorum quam Absiensium, taliter determinaverunt ut omnes haiae et defensabiles habeant universis terris monachorum, circa omnes aquas et rivos, unam hasteam hinc inde. Haiae vero fossatorum habeant large quantum hiatus et aggeres ipsorum, et in terris Vernolii sint ubique convenientes ad mensuram haiarum Guastinae . . ." *Cartulaires de l'Absie,* p. 78.

[74] ". . . videlicet duas sextarias et dimidiam sub Viridario et septem sextarias ad Plantas . . . praeter hec omnia quatuor sextarias terre quam tenebat de Reginaldo de Peirata. . . ." *Cartulaire de Talmond,* p. 171.

of this kind may well have been of the irregular-shaped, open field type with few or no enclosures and with the peasants practicing the *vaine pâture,* although the documents are silent on this last matter.

It was perhaps out beyond the villages in the wilder, more desolate areas where settlements were few and far between, that men, released from the collective restraints of the village, could enclose their newly cleared fields. The layout of the older communities had long been fixed and had to be conformed to, but nothing restricted or limited enclosure in virgin territory. Thus when the lord of Parthenay gave the monks and men of the burg of St. Paul the use of his woods, ". . . ad clausuram burgi et agrorum . . .," he anticipated that the new fields would be enclosed.[75] The enclosure sometimes may have been merely a barrier of dead wood, but in most cases was a hedge, *haia,* of stunted oak trees and bushes. The hedge, which normally grew out of a raised mound of earth flanked by narrow ditches, was of considerable importance in the rural economy of the twelfth century just as it was in the seventeenth century.[76] Not only did it mark off the limits of the *borderia* and keep livestock from invading planted fields, but it furnished firewood at regular intervals when trimmed.

Regions where the enclosed field dominated not only fostered a more individualistic type of farming, but also, as the foregoing pages have emphasized, one which aimed at a high degree of self-sufficiency, with the raising on the land of everything necessary for ordinary needs. It was perfectly natural, indeed imperative, that people who lived more or less isolated in a region with relatively few market towns should avoid depending on others for the necessities of life. Such an economy was not without its advantages in the atmosphere of the twelfth century. Considering the struggle he had in wringing an existence from a barren soil, one must admit that the life of a Gâtinais must have been pretty bleak. Yet when this ability to be self-sufficient is added to the fact that the peasantry were left to themselves and were relatively free from heavy seigneurial exactions, one may very well conclude that there were worse places to have lived in the turbulent eleventh and twelfth centuries.

[75] *Cartuaire de Cormery,* pp. 90–93.
[76] For a detailed description of a hedge see above, p. 40, footnote 73.

CHAPTER II

THE LORDS OF PARTHENAY AND THE GÂTINE

The colonization of the Gâtine was accompanied by a radical alteration in the political and administrative structure of the region which ultimately affected its entire population. The Gâtine was located in the county of Poitou which since 778 had been a part of the kingdom, and later duchy, of Aquitaine and its inhabitants were ruled by the count, an official representative of the Carolingian monarch. In the decades after the year 1000 large parts of the county, including all but a few corners of the Gâtine, gradually escaped the direct control of the count whose authority was weakened by invasions from without and by usurpations of power by his castellans from within. In the Gâtine this development was dominated by the formation of the seigneurial house of Parthenay whose feudal state had come to encompass almost all of that region by the end of the twelfth century. Founded in the turbulent years of the late tenth century, the family of Parthenay rose in spectacular fashion in the eleventh century to become one of the most influential in Poitou. The unchallenged masters of the Gâtine, their reputation spread far beyond the limits of that country in the eleventh and twelfth centuries when they were the much sought after allies of the counts of Poitou and Anjou, the Duke of Normandy in his invasion of England, and the kings of England and France successively. Not until the middle of the thirteenth century, after the decline of the family of Parthenay, was the rule of the count, this time more closely supervised by the French monarchy, once again exercised in the region.

In order to understand how this transformation occurred one must turn to the attacks of Scandinavian peoples against the northern and eastern coasts of France in the ninth century. Striking

42

first in 837 and sporadically thereafter for another 150 years, Viking marauders brought great destruction to the province of Poitou. Although no direct proof of this is available, the Gâtine probably was invaded and devastated to the point that a number of its inhabitants abandoned their homes and fled the region.[1] The continued success of the Vikings demonstrates the weakness of comital government which was incapable of resistance due to internal dynastic strife, lack of assistance from the Carolingian kings, and ineffective defenses. Not until the tenth century, after repeated raids and dreadful losses, did the count solve the problem of defense against the lightning-like incursions of the Norse. Then he had constructed at regular intervals across the province a series of fortifications which provided both rallying points, or places of refuge and protection for the local population, and spots from which counterattacks could be launched.[2] With the re-establishment of some degree of peace and order, the tenth century was one of resurgence of government by the count, although it was now independent of the collapsing monarchy.

Faint but unmistakable traces of this government are visible in parts of the Gâtine in the tenth century. Much of the region was under the jurisdiction of the viscount of Thouars, one of four such delegates appointed by the count in the ninth century to facilitate administration of the province.[3] The northern half of the region was divided into two smaller districts called *vicariae* from the fact that each was ruled by a deputy of the viscount called a *vicarius*.[4] The *vicaria* of Thouars itself extended all the way from Largeasse in the west to Vasles on the southeastern border where it bordered on the *vicaria* of Thénezay.[5] The only

[1] See above, pp. 24–25. A summary of Norse raids in Poitou is presented by Marcel Garaud in " Les incursions des Normands en Poitou et leurs conséquences," *Revue Historique* (1937), pp. 241–68.

[2] On the origins of the Poitevin castles, Marcel Garaud, " L'organisation administrative du comté de Poitou au 10ᵉ siècle et l'avènement des châtelains et des châtellenies," *Bulletin de la société des antiquaires de l'ouest* (1953), pp. 411–54; and Sidney Painter, " Castellans of the Plain of Poitou in the eleventh and twelfth centuries," *Speculum* (1956), pp. 243–57.

[3] Marcel Garaud, " Les vicomtes de Poitou (IXᵉ–XIIᵉ siècles)," *Revue historique du droit français et étranger* (1937), pp. 426 ff.

[4] Garaud, " l'Organisation administrative," pp. 413–33 treats the question of *vicars* and *vicaria*'s in Poitou generally.

[5] *Cartulaire de Talmond*, p. 78; Bibliothèque Nationale, Gaignières, F. L. 17127, p. 263; *Chartes de St. Maixent*, I, 89; *Cartulaire de St. Cyprien*, p. 91.

other reference to a *vicaria* shows that a small sector in the south-west from Coulonges-sur-l'Autize to St. Paul-en-Gâtine was in the *vicaria* of Mervent, belonging directly to the count.[6] The paucity of allusions to the central as well as southern parts of the region forces one to the conclusion that at this early period they were virtually uninhabited and therefore had little need of formal government.

Yet if the castle was a distinct asset to the count in organizing the defense of Poitou, it was at the same time the instrument by which his shaky control over the country was even more seriously threatened. For the same individuals who, as custodians or castellans, had been charged with the command of his various castles quickly discovered that an impregnable stone fortress could be used just as well to resist him as it could to repulse an enemy. They not only withstood the efforts of the count to control them, but within the territory surrounding their fortresses they began to usurp the governmental powers which the latter had failed to exercise. Forcing everyone who lived within the *banlieue* of their castles to accept their police protection and courts of justice, and to pay taxes of various kinds, the feudal castellans began to rule as sovereigns in what became a network of tiny independent states scattered all over Poitou.

What happened in Poitou at large also happened in the Gâtine where a newly constructed castle at Parthenay provided its ruling family with the nucleus for a feudal *seigneurie*, or lordship which eventually grew to include almost all of the region. In the case of some of the Poitevin castles, the builder, the circumstances leading to construction, and its date are known with a fair degree of exactitude, and in a few instances the origin of the castellan himself is known. With regard to Parthenay castle and the lords of Parthenay, however, the scarcity of evidence forces one to resort largely to conjecture.

The first mention of the castle and its lord occurs around 1012 just after Joscelin of Parthenay had died, apparently without an adult heir, leaving his wife and possessions in the custody of the counts of Anjou and Poitou.[7] This is the only indisputable reference to Joscelin I of Parthenay. The same name appears several

---

[6] *Gallia Christiana*, II, Instrumenta, 330.

[7] ". . . Eo tempore accidit ut finiretur de castro Parteniaco Joscelinus, dixitque Comes ut honorem et mulierem eius Hugoni traderet. . ." Besly, *Histoire*, p. 288 bis.

times in the witness lists to charters of the count of Poitou at the end of the tenth and early eleventh centuries, but the customary lack of surnames at that time prevents positive identification with the lord of Parthenay. For instance, the same writer who noted the death of Joscelin of Parthenay also mentioned in the same document another Joscelin, an uncle of Hugh of Lusignan, but only the fact that the lord of Parthenay was already dead makes possible a distinction between the two. Only by supplementing these few inconclusive facts with others from the later history of the family can one begin to penetrate the obscurity surrounding its origins. Stated briefly, the close feudal relationship between the lords of Parthenay and the counts of Anjou and the strong ties between the former and the countries of Anjou and Touraine throughout the eleventh and twelfth centuries plainly hint at an Angevin origin for both the castle and the dynasty despite its location in Poitou. It seems quite likely that Joscelin of Parthenay was a descendant of a noble family of Anjou or the Touraine who, as a vassal of Fulk Nerra, was given recently built Parthenay castle and some of the Gâtine as a fief and thus founded a new Poitevin *seigneurie* around the end of the tenth century.[8]

Whether Joscelin was merely a temporary custodian or had an hereditary claim to be castellan of Parthenay castle is uncertain, as is the size of his estate in the Gâtine. It was clearly large enough to be a major factor in Poitevin politics. For while quarreling with the Viscount of Thouars, Count William of Poitou threatened to give Joscelin's wife and castle to Hugh of Lusignan unless the recalcitrant Viscount came over to his point of view.[9]

---

[8] For a full discussion of this question see Appendix 1. The recent research of K. F. Werner on the origins of the nobility of Anjou and Maine shows that most date back at least to the ninth century and not to the later tenth or early eleventh centuries as previously thought, Karl Werner, "Untersuchungen zur Frühzeit des französichen Fürstentums," *Die Welt als Geschichte* (1958–60), XVIII, 256–89; XIX, 146–93; XX, 87–119. Whether this can be substantiated in the case of the Parthenay family is a moot point. Preliminary paging through sources of Anjou and the Touraine has thus far yielded nothing.

[9] ". . . In hunc vero conventum manduit Hugoni Comes pro Vicecomite Radulfo, dixitque ei: Conventum quod habet tecum Hugo nil illum faciat, quia ego illi prohibeo: sed etiam ego et Fulco conventum habemus ut demus illi honorem et uxorem Joscelini, faciamusque pro tua confusione, quod non es mihi fidelis. Ut audivit Radulfus, dolens fuit valde, et dixit Comiti; Pro Deo tibi sit, non hoc facias: et Comes ait; Fac mihi fiduciam ut non des illi filiam tuam, nec conventum illi attendas, similiterque faciam ut honorem, nec uxorem Joscelini possideat. . . ." Besly, *Histoire*, p. 288 bis.

When the Viscount replied in consternation that he would agree to the terms demanded by his Lord, it was no doubt because he feared that possession of the fief of Parthenay which separated the lands of Thouars and Lusignan would give his adversary an overwhelming advantage in their local wars.

The circumstances under which Joscelin's successor, William I, came to power sometime around 1025 are as problematical as those surrounding his own life. When William I spoke of his father and brothers in a charter of 1039, he did not bother to mention their names, so it is impossible to know if the former was Joscelin of Parthenay.[10] That he should have named his second son Joscelin, however, favors an answer in the affirmative. However, in assessing the importance of William I in feudal Poitou one leaves entirely the realm of probability. Even though of a new family, it is apparent that William was already one of the great noble vassals of the counts of Anjou and Poitou. He often attended those dignitaries at their feudal assemblies and occupied a high position on the list of witnesses to their acts, one time being among a handful of nobles called lords of Aquitain by Pope John XIX.[11] The title *dominus*, or lord, of Parthenay which he appended to his personal name identifies him as a member of an elite class, for only men of castellan rank, or men who held castles and possessed governmental powers over the nearby inhabitants, took this title in eleventh-century France.[12]

[10] *Cartulaire de l'abbaye de Saint-Jean d'Angély* (Georges Musset, ed. Archives historiques de la Saintonge et de l'Aunis, 1901), p. 223.

[11] *Cartulaire de Saint-Jean d'Angély*, I, 32. Auguste Bernard and Alexandre Bruel (eds.), *Recueil des chartes de l'abbaye de Cluny* (Paris, 1888, IV), 610–12. *Cartulaire de St. Cyprien*, 297–98. Alexandre Teulet (ed.), *Layettes du trésor des chartes* (Paris, 1863–66, I), 21a. *Cartulaire de l'abbaye royale de Notre-Dame de Saintes* (T. Grasilier, ed., Cartulaires inédits de la Saintonge, Niort, 1871, II), 5.

[12] Georges Duby, "Une enquête à poursuivre: la noblesse dans la France médiévale," *Revue Historique* (1961), p. 16. Léopold Genicot, "La noblesse au moyen âge dans l'ancienne *Francie.*" *Annales; Économies, Sociétés, Civilisations* (1962), p. 11. Interestingly enough neither the Count of Anjou or the Count of Poitou ever, in the period of this study, used the term when referring in his own charters to a lord of Parthenay, nor for that matter did fellow castellans of approximately the same status. Moreover whenever a lord of Parthenay issued a charter in the presence of the count, he carefully abstained from taking the title *dominus*. Is this simply a matter of deference to a superior or should one conclude that the title *dominus* amounted to a kind of declaration of independence which was best not made in the count's presence? On the other hand vassals of the lord of Parthenay called him *dominus* and *senior* from as early as 1025 whereas churchmen of the province used the term regularly from at least 1090 on.

With considerable ingenuity William utilized wars between the two counts to enhance his own status. Shortly after the death of Count William the Great of Poitou in 1030, his third wife, Agnes, became discontented with the independent manner in which her stepson, William the Fat, began to rule Poitou, and in 1032 she married Geoffrey Martel, the heir apparent to the county of Anjou. Their combined intentions being obviously to oust William the Fat and seize the administration of the province, war quickly broke out and ended in disaster for the Count of Poitou. Taken prisoner at the battle of Montcouer in 1033, he was not released until just before his death in 1038.[13] Lack of information obscures a knowledge of where William of Parthenay stood at that battle, but ensuing events during the continuation of the war prove that he backed the Countess Agnes and the winning cause.

For after the death of William the Fat, his younger brother Odo, Duke of Gascony, became count and attempted to regain control of Poitou. Since Odo's first campaign was aimed at the Gâtine, it is clear that that region was then the stronghold of the Angevin cause in Poitou. A chronicler of the nearby abbey of St. Maixent relates that, after the death of William the Fat, the inhabitants of the Gâtine, with the aid of men from Anjou, built a castle which was under the command of Willam of Parthenay at Germond in the southern part of the region.[14] Since Germond was a village which had long belonged to the counts of Poitou, it is little wonder that Count Odo, upon arriving from Gascony, first struck at his opponents there.[15] His attacks being repulsed, Odo turned south to besiege the castle of Mauzé where he was killed in 1039.[16]

Since the next count of Poitou, William Aigret, or William

---

[13] Alfred Richard, *Histoire des comtes de Poitou* (778–1204) (Paris, 1903, I), 225–34. For the history of the counts of Poitou during the eleventh and twelfth centuries I refer constantly to Richard, supplemented by Louis Halphen, *Le comté d'Anjou au XIᵉ siècle* (Paris, 1906), in questions involving the interrelationships of Anjou and Poitou.

[14] ". . . Eodem tempore Gastinenses Germundum castrum construxerunt, auxilio Andegavorum, Guillelmo Partiniacensium in eodem castro principe. . . ." "Chronicon Sancti-Maxentii Pictavensis," *Chroniques des églises d'Anjou.* Paul Marchegay and Émile Mabille, eds., Société de l'histoire de France (Paris, 1869), p. 392.

[15] *Cartulaire St. Cyprien,* p. 311.

[16] ". . . Interea Odo comes, veniens a Gasconia, voluit capere Germundum castrum, sed non potuit. Inde reversus, Mausiacum . . . occisus est . . ." *Chronicon Sancti-Maxentii Pictavensis,* p. 393.

the Fierce, was a son of Agnes and William the Great, and was in addition a minor, the Countess and Geoffrey Martel were able to govern unchallenged in Poitou for the next eleven years. One of their most prominent vassals was William I of Parthenay who accompanied them on trips far beyond the confines of medieval Poitou. In 1040 in the presence of the King and many feudal princes of western France, he attended the festive consecration ceremony of the famous abbey of the Trinity of Vendôme, thirty-five miles northeast of Tours.[17] In the entourage of three archbishops, six bishops, and eight abbots to mention only the ecclesiastical nobility, he witnessed the foundation of the abbey of Notre Dame de Saintes in the Saintonge in 1047, and in 1049 he was at Angers for the donation of a church of that town to the abbey of Vendôme.[18]

William I of Parthenay died between 1054 and 1058, but before that time he had again changed his allegiance to support the Count of Poitou. Once more the cause was war. When by 1050 Geoffrey Martel, count of Anjou since 1040, had had no children by his much older wife Agnes of Poitou, he renounced her. Agnes returned to Poitiers and hostilities began between the two feudal principalities. After several encounters, neither side had gained a decisive advantage which meant in effect that Angevin influence in Poitevin affairs came to an end. His presence in Poitiers in 1054 when William Aigret, count of Poitou, made gifts to the church of St. Florent of Saumur, shows that William of Parthenay had stayed with Agnes and her son and supported the victorious party.[19]

William emerged from these wars not only on the winning side but also in possession of a second castle at Germond to strengthen his control of the Gâtine. But that control was far from complete for shortly thereafter Germond somehow reverted to the Count of Poitou, whereas another nobleman, Simon of Verruyes, ruled substantial parts of the remainder of the region. In addition to holding Verruyes and several other estates in the southeastern Gâtine, Simon was almost certainly lord of Hérisson

[17] *Layettes du trésor des chartes*, I, 21a.

[18] *Cartulaire de Saintes*, II, 5. *Cartulaire de Vendôme*, II, 164–68.

[19] *Chartes poitevines de l'abbaye de Saint-Florent, près de Saumur* (Paul Marchegay, ed., Archives historiques du Poitou, II), 93.

castle located about ten miles west of Parthenay.[20] It is quite possible that an unknown episode in the war which occupied William of Parthenay and the Count of Poitou near Germond gave him an opportunity to build this castle which is mentioned for the first time shortly after 1040. In any event the possession of Hérisson and the other lands gave Simon a sudden prominence during the fifth decade of the eleventh century when he appeared at several of the feudal assemblies of the Countess Agnes, her son William, count of Poitou and her husband Geoffrey, count of Anjou, along with some of their leading vassals such as the lords of Vouvent, Parthenay, Montreuil-Bellay, and the family of Rancon.[21] From the extent of Simon's lands to the south and west of Parthenay it can easily be appreciated that William of Parthenay did not dominate much more than the central and northeastern parts of the Gâtine which lay in the shadow of his castle.

His possessions were centered in the Gâtine but William I had a number of estates in Bas-Poitou to the west and in the marsh of Poitou to the south. The existence of lands belonging to him at places like Vix, la Piraire and St. Hilaire-de-Riez is revealed only because he donated part or all of them to monasteries, so one may suspect that he had more in reserve.[22] With the exception of what seems to have been an allod at Fontaines these estates were fiefs held from the count of Poitou and the viscount of Thouars, a fact which helps explain how the lord of Parthenay acquired them. Faced at the end of the tenth century by the depopulated wastes of Bas-Poitou, Count William the Great of Poitou may well have assigned large sections of this country to certain of his vassals located nearby for the purpose of resettling and defending it. On the other hand William of Parthenay stated quite specifically that he received the domaine of la Piraire in the Saintonge as a gift from a Countess Adele of the family of Anjou, perhaps, one may speculate, as a reward for his fidelity to the Angevin cause from 1032-50.[23]

---

[20] *Chartes de St. Maixent*, I, 120-21.

[21] *Layettes du trésor des chartes*, I, 20-21. *Cartulaire de Vendôme*, I, 42-44. *Cartulaire saintongeais de la Trinité de Vendôme* (Charles Metais, ed., Archives historiques de la Saintonge et de l'Aunis, 1893), pp. 43-45.

[22] *Cartulaire de St. Cyprien*, p. 339. *Cartulaire de Saintes*, II, 143-44. *Cartulaire de St. Jean d'Angély*, I, 223.

[23] ". . . ego, Vuillelmus cum consilio et consensu domnae comitissae Agnetis filiorumque eius . . . dono . . . quamdam villulam atque curticulam parvam, Pirariis

William of Parthenay fulfilled with great skill his obligations to provide for his children and thereby considerably aggrandized his family standing among the Poitevin nobility. A vexing problem for a medieval noble was always posed by several daughters who all needed marriage dowries. William and his wife apparently had only one, Beatrice, and she, as a very young girl, was placed as a nun in the newly founded convent at Saintes.[24] His eldest son and heir, William II, was married and had two sons by 1047, but it is impossible to identify the family of his wife.[25] Profiting from his Angevin contacts in the Saintonge, William I arranged for the marriage of his fourth son Gelduin to the heiress of the house of Tonnay-Boutonne shortly after 1047.[26] Gelduin and his heirs became the lords of this castle east of La Rochelle and remained in close alliance with the family of Parthenay during the next one hundred fifty years as will become clearer in the following pages. It may also be presumed that William I planned the union between his third son, Simon, and Milesend, a daughter of Hugh V of Lusignan, even though their marriage did not take place until after his death.[27] But William I's greatest accomplishment was in obtaining a high position in the church for his

nomine, quam possedi ex dono domnae Adthelae, comitissae. . ." *Cartulaire de St. Jean d'Angély,* I, 223. William, in other words, donated this *domaine* which had been given to him by a Countess Adèle, at the advice of Agnes, countess of Poitou, and wife of Geoffrey Martel. But who is the Countess Adèle? Paul Marchegay, *Notice sur les archevêques, anciens seigneurs de Parthenay* (no date or place of publication on the copy in the Bibliothèque Municipale of Poitiers), p. 153, equates her with the Countess Aumode, the first wife of Count William the Great of Poitou. Yet this is impossible for two reasons; the Countess Aumode was known by that name and not Adèle, and further, she died around 1005 (Richard, *Histoire des comtes de Poitou,* I, 169) when William of Parthenay would have been a baby if even born. The most satisfactory explanation is that she was Adèle, a daughter of Fulk Nerra, who by marriage and inheritance became Countess of Vendôme around 1016. It was through her marriage that the counts of Anjou came to exercise considerable influence in the county of Vendôme for several decades in the early eleventh century. (Halphen, *Le comté d'Anjou,* p. 60.) When loyal to the Angevin cause, William of Parthenay was frequently north of the Loire River and was at least once in Vendôme for the consecration of the new abbey in 1040. It was probably at this time that he made the acquaintance of Adèle and somehow received gifts from her.

[24] *Cartulaire de Saintes,* II, 143–44.

[25] *Ibid.*

[26] *Ibid.*

[27] Simon was married to Milesind before 1068. Bibliothèque Nationale, Gaignières, F. L. 17127, p. 379. The fact that their son, Simon II, lord of Parthenay from 1110–21, was the nephew of Hugh VI of Lusignan shows that Milesind was the daughter of Hugh V, and a sister of Hugh VI, *Chartes de St. Maixent,* I, 276.

second son, Joscelin. His office as treasurer of the influential abbey of St. Hilaire of Poitiers, whose abbot was the Count of Poitou, was to lead Joscelin to a distinguished ecclesiastical career.[28]

When William I died, between 1054 and 1058, leaving a *seigneurie* firmly established and a family well provided for, he was survived by five sons born of his wife Arengarde. By 1047 his eldest son, William junior, had been designed as his heir and William had proceeded to obtain the office of treasurer in the abbey of St. Hilaire for Joscelin, his second son. When William junior died unexpectedly sometime between 1049 and 1054 his father realized that under the prevailing custom his *seigneurie* would fall to his eldest grandson, then only a child. Foreseeing the dire consequences of the rule of a minor, William I turned to his next son, Joscelin. Since the first act issued after William's death was in the name of his third son, Simon, as well as that of Joscelin, one must infer that William had appointed those two as co-rulers of the Parthenay, apparently from fear that the latter's ecclesiastical duties would occupy too much of his time.[29] William I thus adopted and persuaded his sons to continue after his death a new system of inheritance called the *droit de viage ou retour*. According to this custom the principle of primogeniture, with the eldest son inheriting nearly all the patrimony, was strictly enforced except for one drastic modification. When the eldest son died the administration of the inheritance passed intact into the hands of his next oldest brother instead of devolving upon his oldest son. This process continued with each of his brothers in turn governing the family holdings, and not until they were all dead was the patrimony returned in its entirety to the first son of the eldest brother. The advantages of this system are obvious. It was more equitable for younger brothers, it maintained the inheritance intact at all times, and finally it practically insured the administration of a mature individual and not a helpless minor, such as happened when a father died leaving only infant sons.[30]

In 1059 came an event of extraordinary good fortune for the

[28] Joscelin became treasurer before 1047. *Cartulaire de Saintes*, II, 143–44.

[29] *Cartulaire de Saintes*, II, 145.

[30] The lords of Parthenay were among the first noble families of Poitou to have instituted this unusual system of inheritance which is found nowhere else in medieval France. The most authoritative discussion of the subject is an article of Marcel Garaud entitled " Le viage ou le retour du vieux coustumier de Poictou," *Bulletin de la société des antiquaires de l'ouest* (1921), pp. 747–800.

family, the appointment of Joscelin as archbishop of Bordeaux. Joscelin's election to this high office was apparently related to the accession of a new count of Poitou, Guy-Geoffrey, in that same year. No sooner had he come to power than the Count deposed the incumbent archbishop, Archembaud—a native of the Gâtine incidentally—and replaced him with the lord of Parthenay. Joscelin probably made his spectacular advance to the top of the Poitevin church hierarchy because he was treasurer of St. Hilaire of Poitiers, an office which had put him in the constant company of the Count of Poitou, the titular abbot of the same monastery.[31] For nearly thirty years thereafter Joscelin's activities turned more and more to the absorbing question of the Gregorian church reforms, which demanded that he preside over numerous provincial church councils and travel frequently, including at least one trip to Rome. Although he was usually an advocate for papal reform measures Joscelin's fame in Poitevin and ecclesiastical history derives perhaps more from his sometimes doubtful religious orthodoxy. He was a firm friend of the heretic Berenger of Tours and more than once was reprimanded for adherence to the latter's unacceptable beliefs.[32]

Until becoming archbishop of Bordeaux in 1059, Joscelin administered the temporal affairs of the Parthenay land conjointly with his brother Simon in spite of his other obligations as treasurer of St. Hilaire. Even after 1059 with his enormously increased burdens as prelate of northern Aquitaine he managed to keep in touch with his barony. Yet it was inevitable that his brother Simon would gradually assume more responsibility in the supervision of the family patrimony and that his relationship to Joscelin would be more clearly defined. That this in fact happened stands out unmistakably in the foundation charters for the burgs of Secondigny around 1068, and St. Paul of Parthenay slightly later. In the first instance Joscelin entitled himself simply archbishop of Bordeaux, and Simon, " my brother and regent of my castle of Parthenay." [33] Simon had acquired more authority a bit later when, as lord—*dominus*—of Parthenay castle, he

[31] Richard, *Histoire des comtes de Poitou*, I, 275–76.

[32] *Ibid.*, pp. 315–17.

[33] ". . . Ego Goscelinus archiepiscopus Burdegalensis urbis Simon que frater meus Partiniacensis Castri mei vice-dominus. . . ." Bibliothèque Nationale, Gaignières, F. L. 17127, p. 379.

granted land and privileges to the abbey of St. Paul of Cormery leaving his elder brother Joscelin merely to authenticate the charter as lord—*senior*—of the honor of Parthenay.[34]

Simon, however, died prematurely between 1070–74 and Joscelin was compelled to appoint a successor. Following the example of his father, Joscelin continued to associate his brothers in the direction of the Parthenay lands, but instead of his next eldest he chose his youngest brother, Ebbo, a move which was to have drastic consequences later when a fratricidal war broke out among the latter two. Joscelin's motives in preferring Ebbo to his older brother, Gelduin, could well have been that since the latter's marriage around 1050 into the family of Tonnay-Boutonne in the Saintonge, he had become lord of that castle and was occupied in running its affairs. However, Ebbo, the fifth and youngest son of William I had no external obligations through marriage and was free to devote full time to the administration of the barony. Thus it was he who represented the house of Parthenay in a feudal assembly of the Count of Poitou at Maillezais in 1074.[35] Ebbo's position was not strong enough to pass unchallenged for in a charter of 1078 both he and Gelduin appeared as co-rulers with their brother the archbishop.[36]

In marked contrast to the preceding one, the thirty year period of Joscelin's rule (1058–86) was marred by few major wars in Poitou. The dormant conflict of the counts of Anjou and Poitou was awakened only in two isolated campaigns in 1061–62 and 1068, whereby, Guy-Geoffrey of Poitou succeeded in ousting his opponent from the Saintonge.[37] The silence of chroniclers on the subject and the absence of the name Parthenay from the feudal assemblies of the Count of Anjou cause one to suspect that that family was no longer siding with their former suzerain. Instead his duties as ecclesiastical prelate and as treasurer of St. Hilaire made Archbishop Joscelin the constant companion and close friend

---

[34] ". . . praesente quoque et auctorizante Simone domino Parthenaci castri . . . Hanc cartam legit per semetipsum dominus Gauscelinus Burdegalensis archiepiscopus, senior honoris Parthenaci, legit, concessit, firmavit, et auctorizavit. . . ." *Cartulaire de Cormery*, pp. 90–93.

[35] L'abbé Lacurie, *Histoire de l'abbaye de Maillezais* (Fontenay-le-Comte, 1852), p. 218.

[36] Paul Marchegay (ed.), *Cartulaires du Bas-Poitou* (Les Roches-Baritaud, 1877), p. 92.

[37] Richard, *Histoire des comtes de Poitou*, I, 285.

of the Count of Poitou. Certainly the most warlike event of
Joscelin's rule was the participation of the family of Parthenay
in the conquest of England in 1066. Simon of Parthenay was one
of the most notable of the large contingent of Poitevin nobles
who fought for Duke William of Normandy under the leadership
of the Viscount of Thouars.[38]

Profiting from their harmonious relations with the Count of
Poitou from 1058–86 the Lord of Parthenay and his brothers made
great progress in the internal development of their barony. They
played no small part in the movement of recolonization then
taking place by granting exemptions from sales and road taxes
in order to encourage people to live and trade in the several new
burgs founded in and around Parthenay. It was at that time that
Parthenay ceased to be merely a military outpost and became a
town of some industry and trade. Indeed by the end of the
eleventh century the new woolen industry had prospered to such
an extent that cloths of Parthenay had acquired renown in places
well beyond the confines of the Gâtine.[39]

During the reign of Joscelin an important move was made
toward expanding the barony into the western Gâtine by the
construction of a castle at Secondigny, nine miles west of Parthenay. Possession of the castle at Secondigny, whose existence is
first brought to light by an incidental reference in the charter of
foundation of its burg, not only enabled the lords of Parthenay
to extend their control over the inhabitants in that part of the
Gâtine, but also protected Parthenay from attack from that
direction.[40]

The charter of 1068 does not reveal who had custody of
Secondigny for the lord of Parthenay but only speaks abstractedly
of the prince, *Princeps*, of the castle. From his position at the
head of the list of witnesses to the charter one surmises that
Joscelin's nephew, Odo, the son of Gelduin of Tonnay-Boutonne,
held that post in 1068.[41] If this were the case, however, it was

---

[38] *Revue Anglo-Française*, I (1833), 39.

[39] A transaction in St. Jean d'Angély in the Saintonge in 1097 involved some
cloth from Parthenay. ". . . quinque ulnas de panno que dicitur de Partiniaco. . . ."
Cartulaire de St. Jean d'Angély, I, 150. See below, p. 123, footnote 80.

[40] Bibliothèque Nationale, Gaignières, F. L. 17127, p. 379.

[41] Further support for this belief came from the fact that the twelfth-century
descendants of this same Gelduin held land and rights in and around Secondigny.
Documents inédits sur le département des Deux-Sèvres (Mémoires de la société de

only a temporary appointment since Odo never again figured in charters concerning Secondigny and in 1092 was living in Parthenay.[42] In the later eleventh and twelfth centuries two families were prominent in affairs dealing with Secondigny and in 1111 it is fairly certain that Geoffrey Fulchard was custodian in fact if not in name. For when Mainard the Limousin gave a field of one-half a *borderia* close to Secondigny to his nephew, the latter was required to go to the castle and swear fidelity to the lords of the land. It was Geoffrey Fulchard who received his oath.[43] Nevertheless it is noteworthy that no one called himself lord of that castle. This rather curious anonymity may be the result of incomplete documentation, but it may also reflect a deliberate and astute policy of the lords of Parthenay to maintain direct control over the castle by preventing anyone from claiming an exclusive and hereditary right to that office.

Immediately after Joscelin's death the close co-operation with the Count which had accompanied his rule gave way to a series of destructive baronial wars between the Count of Poitou and the lords of Parthenay which lasted on and off for thirty years. For almost twenty years the lords of Parthenay succeeded in winning and defying the mighty Count, but then the capture of first the lord and then his principal castle cancelled most of their gains and left the family firmly in check. A family quarrel over the matter of succession seems to have precipitated the struggle. When Archbishop Joscelin passed over Gelduin, the logical successor to Simon as the co-ruler of the Parthenay *domaines*, in favor of his younger brother Ebbo, as early as 1074 he may have antagonized the former.[44] Gelduin did not accept relegation to the background, but forced his brother the archbishop to recognize him as dual administrator with Ebbo. According to the family custom Gelduin should have succeeded alone after Joscelin's

---

statistique, sciences, lettres et arts du départment des Deux-Sèvres, 2nd series, XIV, 1875), 284–86. Archives de Maine-et-Loire, Série 187H1, No. 1. Around 1180 Duke Richard of Aquitaine gave Ralph of Tonnay the castle of Secondigny which he had confiscated from the Lord of Parthenay. *Rotuli Litterarum Patentium*. T. Duffus Hardy, ed., Record Commission (London, 1835, I), 11.

[42] *Cartulaire de Talmond*, pp. 175–76.

[43] ". . . Hoc fuit factum Segundiniaco castellulo, in domo Giraudi Charmenol, et ibidem promisit fidem suam Airaudus, nepos meus, se hoc tenendo, me vidente et fratre suo Bernardo, Goffredo Fulchardo qui fidem suam accepit. . . ." *Chartes de St. Maixent*, I, 276.

[44] See above, p. 53.

death in 1086, but a charter of a year later, in which Gelduin and Ebbo were named twin lords of Parthenay, disclosed that Ebbo would not relinquish the power he had once tasted.[45] There followed three or four years when first one then the other was referred to as the lord of Parthenay, a fact which merely reflects the confusion in the minds of contemporary observers, and which hints at the struggle for predominance within the family. In 1092 Ebbo seems to have gained the upper hand and forced his brother to leave the Gâtine, for in 1093 Gelduin took the step, which later proved disastrous, of appealing to the Count of Poitou for aid. As the feudal superior of the lords of Parthenay the young count, William the Troubadour, had the right of intervening to assure proper succession to his vassal's fiefs, but up until this point had kept clear of the strife. The death of Archbishop Joscelin at the same time as that of Count Guy-Geoffrey had left the traditionally close relationship between the two houses in a state of uncertainty, and in Gelduin's invitation Count William may well have seen an opportunity to profit from fraternal dissension and retain a hand in the affairs of the vital frontier barony.

Since the dispute continued one must presume that Ebbo was undaunted by the Count's intervention and decided to defy him. After all William was only sixteen years old when he came to power and completely untried in feudal politics and war. Appearances of Ebbo of Parthenay at the feudal court of Aimery, viscount of Thouars, after 1088 suggest that he had turned for aid to his powerful northern neighbors in order to counterbalance the influence of the count of Poitou in the case of conflict.[46]

From 1091 to 1093 the Gâtine was the scene of preparation for an anticipated war, and once again as in 1037–39 there was activity in the strategically vital southern part of the region. By 1091 a castle had been erected at Ternant about thirteen miles south of Parthenay and five miles northeast of Germond.[47] Commanding Ternant was a certain Ermengodus, a follower of Gervais of Verruyes, who was one of the strongest vassals of the lords of Parthenay in the southern Gâtine. Gervais of Verruyes,

---

[45] ". . . Necnon domini de opido Parthenay videlicet Gelduinus et Ebo. . ." *Cartulaire du prieuré de Saint Nicolas de Poitiers* (Louis Redet, ed., Archives historiques du Poitou, 1872), p. 19.

[46] MSS Dom Fonteneau, XXVI, 163. Bibliothèque Nationale, Gaignières, F. L. 17127, p. 173.

[47] *Chartes de St. Maixent*, I, 211.

whose ancestor Simon was encountered earlier as the castellan of Hérisson castle, himself held a fortified tower, *mota*, next to the church of Verruyes.[48] The third place to be fortified within a very few years time was Germond. In the interval between 1039, when William I of Parthenay had built and successfully defended it, and 1087, Germond castle had somehow been razed or neglected and returned to the Count, for at the latter date William the Troubadour regranted privileges to its villagers which went back to the year 1003. The original grant contained only one new clause, but that was a significant one: in case of war the inhabitants would be required to fight and aid in beseiging castles. Anticipating trouble, Count William had taken measures to insure that he would have an army in case of need. The castle at Germond was not rebuilt until 1093 when it served as a base of operations for Gelduin of Parthenay and his ally the Count after the former had been exiled from the Gâtine by his brother Ebbo.[49] No doubt considering it an intolerable threat to his safety, Ebbo of Parthenay attacked and destroyed the new castle at an opportune moment in 1094 when Count William was in the south of France.[50] Since nothing is heard of him after 1094 one may presume that Gelduin was killed in this battle leaving Ebbo to rule the Parthenay domains unchallenged.

Occupied with his marriage to a princess in Toulouse and with preparations for a coming crusade William the Troubadour accepted the defeat of his protégé Gelduin without attempting a reprisal, and the war lapsed for several years. Ebbo of Parthenay apparently took advantage of this period of calm to go on the first crusade, but seems to have returned before Jerusalem was taken in 1099.[51] Then in 1100 the Count of Poitou himself, who

---

[48] ". . . et mota qui est juxta ecclesiam Verruce, cum stagno. . . ." *Ibid.*, p. 210. Whether this *mota* had any great military value is doubtful since in this same act Gervais gave it to the Abbey of St. Maixent.

[49] ". . . MLXXXXIII; Germundum castrum factum est, causa contentionis Gelduini et Ebbonis fratrum, a Guillelmo comite et eodem Gelduino. . . ." *Chronicon Sancti-Maxentii Pictavensis*, p. 410.

[50] ". . . MLXXXXIV; Germundum destructum est. . . ." *Ibid.* It was probably during a preliminary skirmish in 1093 that Guy of Ternant was captured and ransomed by the monks of St. Maixent. *Chartes de St. Maixent*, I, 213.

[51] Ledain, *La Gâtine*, p. 53. Ebbo had returned to Poitou sometime before December, 1099, at which time he witnessed the foundation of the church of Chaise-le-Vicomte in Bas-Poitou. Paul Marchegay (ed.), *Cartulaires du Bas-Poitou* (Les Roches-Baritaud, 1877), p. 344.

had managed to avoid going with the first crusaders took up the cross. It was after his return from a brief sojourn of eighteen months in the Holy Land that the conflict between the Count and Ebbo of Parthenay was renewed. On this occasion their quarrel was only a part of a larger dispute involving the Count of Anjou as well. It began when Geoffrey Martel, son of Fulk, the count of Anjou, revolted successfully from his father and led an expedition into the Saintonge attempting to recover the former Angevin fiefs there which the count of Poitou, Guy-Geoffrey, had confiscated in 1068.[52] As had been customary in the eleventh century the Angevin army passed into the Saintonge by way of the Gâtine, whose ruler, the Lord of Parthenay, once again supported the Count of Anjou. Count William of Poitou sought to frustrate this campaign by invading the Gâtine and placing his men across the path of the returning Angevin host. The two armies confronted each other in 1104 at Parthenay where only torrential rains and a subsequent truce rather mysteriously prevented what could have been a major disaster for Ebbo of Parthenay.[53] This was the last episode in the wars opposing William the Troubadour and Ebbo of Parthenay who died in 1110.

At this point the house of Parthenay was stronger than ever. The Count's castle at Germond had been destroyed definitively whereas two new castles fortified their grip on the Gâtine. In addition to the castle at Ternant they now commanded one at Champdeniers which guarded the vulnerable southern flank of the region. In all probability Ebbo decided to replace Germond with Champdeniers three miles to the north rather than rebuild on the old controversial site.[54] With the addition of Champdeniers to the fortifications at Parthenay and Secondigny, the barony of Parthenay took its definitive medieval form of three major castles and two minor ones (Ternant and Hérisson), a structure which was not to be modified, and then not basically, until the early thirteenth century. Moreover that barony now comprised most

---

[52] See above, p. 53.

[53] ". . . MCIV; in pictavia civitate oppressio bellorum, nam praeparatum fuit maximum bellum inter Willelmum, comitem Pictavorum et Guoffredum Martellum, filium Fulconis Andegavorum, VI nonas novembris, apud Partiniacum; sed Dominus per bonos et sanctos viros placitavit et pluviam magnam ubertim, per duos dies et noctes, assidue cadere permisit. . . ." *Chronicon Sancti-Maxentii Pictavensis*, p. 422.

[54] The castle at Champdeniers is first mentioned in 1111. *Chronicon Sancti-Maxentii Pictavensis*, p. 425.

of the Gâtine, for in 1111, a year after Ebbo's death, a monk of St. Maixent referred to the new head of the family as Simon of the Gâtine, and not just Simon of Parthenay.[55]

In several respects Ebbo of Parthenay resembles quite closely the kind of independent feudal baron one might imagine to have been typical of the eleventh century. At the same time that he boldly defied his feudal suzerain, the Count of Poitou, he cowed his vassals in the Gâtine with a ferocity which left a singular impression on their minds.[56] In his relations with the church Ebbo displayed a fine combination of belligerence and piety tempered by considerations of practicability. On the one hand he allowed his vassals to oppress the priory of la Peyratte until in desperation the Abbot of St. Croix of Talmond was forced to pay the Lord of Parthenay heavily to protect his priory.[57] On the other hand he treated with great partiality certain churches which had gained or bought his favor. As the *advocatus* or protector, of the monastery of Luçon (which was located in a fief belonging to the family of Parthenay) he became involved in a series of violent wars with the abbey of St. Michel-en-l'Herm in order to safeguard the right of the former institution.[58] Nonetheless striking were Ebbo's acts of largess to the priory of Parthenay-le-Vieux, and he was probably also the builder of several churches in Parthenay, including a most unusual church-in-the-round.[59]

Under his successors victory turned to defeat and eventually the loss of the war. The accession in 1110 or 1111 of Simon II, who was the son of either Simon I (1058–74) or Ebbo himself, was very likely the occasion for the resumption of hostilities with the Count.[60] This supposition is strengthened by the fact that

[55] *Chartes de St. Maixent*, I, 273. Not until around 1240 did a lord of Parthenay equate his barony with the Gâtine. At that time William IV wrote about some acquisitions ". . . in terra nostra de Vastina. . . ." MSS Dom Fonteneau, I, 391–99.

[56] The case of Guy of Vaucouleurs is a convincing example. See below, p. 79.

[57] ". . . Hanc pactionem et conventionem fecit predictus abbas in manu domini Ebonis, et propter hoc dedit abbas domino Eboni VI libras denariorum Andegavorum, ut ipse eamdem terram et quidquid in eodem regione habebat sub custodia sua deffenderet. . . ." *Cartulaire de Talmond*, p. 173.

[58] Bibliothèque Nationale, *Collection Dupuy*, Vol. 499, fol. 17, verso. This is a copy of a charter of Bishop Peter II of Poitiers.

[59] Besly, *Histoire*, p. 396. Modeled after the Church of the Holy Sepulchre in Jerusalem, this church may have been inspired by his crusade to the Holy Land. Ledain, *La Gâtine*, p. 54.

[60] Since Ebbo was the last of the sons of William I, the administration of the

Simon's uncle and staunch ally, Hugh VI of Lusignan, succeeded
his father as lord of Lusignan and was drawn into war with the
Count of Poitou at precisely the same time. As in 1039 and 1094
the southern Gâtine was once again the scene for this chapter
of the war which broke out with great brutality in 1111.[61] And
as in 1039 the Lord of Parthenay called upon the Count of Anjou
for assistance. However, not even an Angevin garrison reinforcing
the castle of Champdeniers could prevent William the Troubadour
from invading the southern Gâtine and laying waste to the country
around Ternant.[62] Nothing is known about the outcome of the
hostilities begun in 1111, but they were probably indecisive since
in 1118 the Count again was warring with Hugh and Simon who
no longer had Angevin support. This time at an unknown place
he routed the armies of both and captured Simon in addition.[63]
Then when scarcely out of captivity, Simon met with a sudden
and mysterious death in Parthenay in 1121, presumably having
been murdered.[64] Since Simon II had no younger brothers the
lordship of Parthenay passed to his eldest son, William II, whose

barony, in accordance with the *droit de viage*, was to revert to the first male heir
of the latter's eldest son, William II. However, neither of the two sons of William
II, Hugh and William, whose existence is known from their presence as witnesses
to charters of 1047 and 1058, in fact became lord of Parthenay, but that position
was in the hands of Simon II after 1111. (*Cartulaire de Saintes*, II, 143–44, 145.
Chartes de St. Maixent, I, 273.) Lacking a better explanation one must assume that
both Hugh and William died without heirs, causing the succession to pass to the
second son of Simon I, the co-ruler of Parthenay with Archbishop Joscelin from
1058–74. Simon's eldest son William was bypassed in favor of Simon II apparently
because the former had been given the post of treasurer of St. Hilaire of Poitiers
after the demise of his uncle, Achbishop Joscelin, in 1086. (*Documents de St.
Hilaire*, I, 106–7.)

[61] The war of 1111 made such an impression on the monks of the nearby abbey
of St. Maixent that at three separate times during that year they noted it down,
utterly out of context, in charters having nothing to do with the Gâtine. *Chartes de
St. Maixent*, I, 242, 272–73, 275–76.

[62] ". . . Andegavini fuerunt in exercitu castello Campolinario. . . ." *Chronicon
Sancti-Maxentii Pictavensis*, p. 425. Count William's campaign had such disastrous
effects on Ternant that the village seems to have become an abandoned site from the
twelfth century on. Houses and land were burnt and in all probability the castle
of Ternant was destroyed for it never again was mentioned in contemporary records.
". . . Guillelmo comite, qui ipsam (houses and land) combusrat propter guerram
Hugonis Liziniaci et cognati sui Simonis de Gastina. . . ." *Chartes de St. Maixent*,
I, 272–73.

[63] ". . . Comes pugnavit cum Simone Partiniacensi et avunculo suo Hugone:
V idus augusti devicit eos et Simonem cepit cum multis aliis. . . ." *Chronicon
Sancti-Maxentii Pictavensis*, p. 428.

[64] ". . . Simon mortuus est Partiniaco, morte subitanea. . . ." *Ibid.*, p. 430.

assumption of power brought a renewal of fighting. The Count of Poitou invaded the Gâtine, laid seige to and finally took Parthenay castle in 1122 and William II's only consolation for an otherwise crushing defeat was that he was able to escape the humiliation of being captured.[65] Thus for the first time in almost a century Parthenay castle was at the disposal of the Count of Poitou. However unfortunate this may have been for the family of Parthenay it is certain that it meant a measure of relief for the peasants of the Gâtine who had been afflicted with almost forty years of intermittent fighting, violent death, and destruction of their lands.

However important the factors of leadership and fighting ability may have been, and evidence on the subject is totally lacking, the explanation for the reversal and defeat of the lords of Parthenay certainly must derive in large part from the greater wealth and man power of the count. Resistance and even temporary success were possible on occasion, but a permanent victory over an opponent of that stature was out of the question. The lords of Parthenay made a miscalculation.

There is a striking lack of information about some phases of the history of the family of Parthenay after 1122. In contrast with the earlier period, fewer of their personal charters have survived. They appeared much less frequently as witnesses or participants in the affairs of other Poitevin or Angevin nobility and seem to have abandoned almost entirely the great feudal assemblies of the counts of Anjou and Poitou.[66] Finally neighboring monastic chroniclers who often recorded their activities in the eleventh and early twelfth centuries completely ignored or lost sight of them in the later twelfth century. In part this must be attributed simply to the well-known relative scarcity of documentation for Poitevin history at that time.[67] And yet mo-

---

[65] "... MCXXII 3 kalendas aprilis, subactum est castrum Partiniacum a Guillelmo comite. ..." *Ibid.*, p. 430. William II of Parthenay took refuge at Bressuire after the fall of his own castle. *Mémoires de la société de statistique des Deux-Sèvres*, 2nd series, XIV (1875), 284–86.

[66] The lords of Parthenay are known to have appeared at such an assembly only once after 1122. *Cartulaires de l'Absie*, pp. 87–88. However caution is necessary here since they may have been among the unnamed barons of Aquitaine to answer the periodic summons of Henry II in the 1150's and 1160's. J. Boussard, *Le Gouvernement d'Henri II Plantagenêt* (Paris, 1956), pp. 409, 416, 419 ff.

[67] S. Painter, "Castellans of the Plain of Poitou in the eleventh and twelfth centuries," p. 257.

nastic charters contain a substantial amount of material on their government of the Gâtine. In view of this it seems unavoidable that in part at least the silence of the sources reflects a withdrawal of the family from the main currents of Poitevin politics. Whereas earlier they were prominent in affairs throughout the province and beyond, now they seem to have become nobles of primarily local importance. Moreover within the Gâtine where they were the acknowledged masters the earlier movement of expansion gradually came to a halt. After 1122 they built no new castles or burgs and acquired little new land. Thus decline in regional importance on the one hand and territorial containment on the other were the outstanding characteristics of the history of the Parthenays during most of the twelfth century. Can there be any hesitation in interpreting these as the aftereffects of the defeats of 1118 and 1122 and the continuing growth of comital government?

Due to the peculiar nature of the documentation for this period it is much more difficult to portray the lords of Parthenay from 1122–82 as historical personalities than their eleventh-century predecessors. In fact so little is known about them as individuals that there is uncertainty as to whether two or three William's ruled during those six decades.[68] It was William II who, after succeeding his father Simon in 1122, adopted the rather incongruous cognomen, archbishop, *Archiepiscopus*, thus beginning a custom which died out only with the line in the fifteenth century. It is not difficult to imagine that William II, witnessing the low ebb of his family's fortune during the wars of Simon II and the Count of Poitou, attempted to restore some of its lost prestige by reviving the use of a title borne by his most distinguished ancestor, Archbishop Joscelin of Bordeaux.[69]

In 1129 William joined a rebellion of Angevin and Poitevin barons against the new count of Anjou, Geoffrey the Fair.[70]

---

[68] Without listing his sources, Marchegay, *Notice sur les archevêques, anciens seigneurs de Parthenay*, decided that there were three rulers named William from 1122–82, whereas Ledain, *La Gâtine*, p. 67, concluded that there were only two. The latter choice is more acceptable but there is no way of proving its validity beyond question.

[69] Despite the fact that the title was quite inappropriate most contemporaries seem to have been impressed by its novelty and monastic scribes took care to record the full title, *Guillelmus archiepiscopus dominus Parteniacensis*, in their charters.

[70] ". . . Verum quia, ut assolet novis rebus antequam convalescent infertur pernicies barones ejus (Comes Gaufridus) Guido de Lavalle, Giraudus Briais, Toarcensis, Mirebellensis, Ambaziacensis, Partiniacensis, Sabaliensis et multi alii perduellionem

Having replaced his father, Fulk the Young, who had just left for the Holy Land, Count Geoffrey was every bit equal to the occasion and put down the uprising in emphatic fashion by seizing the stronghold of the opposition. When William II saw Thouars castle taken and partially destroyed and an army of the Count of Anjou marching on Parthenay he sued for peace.[71] The lesson of 1122 was still fresh in his mind. The motives for William's participation in this revolt are obscure. Perhaps it was revenge for the failure of the Count of Anjou to support him in the wars of 1118 and 1122. In any event it represents a break from the traditional policy of his family with regard to the Count of Anjou.

A political change of the first order occurred in Poitou in 1137 when Louis, son of Louis VI and heir to the French throne, became duke of Aquitaine and count of Poitou through marriage to Eleanor, daughter and heiress of Duke William the Toulousain. Immediately after his marriage Louis became king of France, but being fully occupied with royal affairs spent little time in Poitou.[72]

Then in 1152 Eleanor of Aquitaine quite unexpectedly divorced Louis VII and married Henry Plantagenêt of the comital house of Anjou, making the latter the duke of Aquitaine. After becoming king of England as well in 1154, Henry II showed no inclination to neglect his continental lands and made frequent expeditions there during the thirty-five years of his reign. Henry's harsh punitive policies against the unruly nobility of Aquitaine incurred their deep hostility and when his sons Richard and Henry, with Louis VII of France, led a major revolt against him in 1172–73 a number of them were quick to support it. One of the few facts known about William III of Parthenay, who ruled from sometime between 1159 and 1169 and 1182, is that he was one of the rebels.[73] After a year of sporadic fighting, Henry slowly reduced

meditati sunt, et adversus dominum novum in mentis incude veteri nova machinamenta cudere coeperunt. . . ." *Chroniques des comtes d'Anjou*. Paul Marchegay and André Salmon, eds., Société de l'histoire de France (Paris, 1856–71), p. 263.

[71] ". . . Amoto inde exercitu, Parteniacum, injuriae gratia ulciscendae proficiscitur. Parteniensis vero dominus, per internuncios rogat quae ad pacem sunt; et facta deditione a liberalitatis principia pacem et gratiam optatam assecutus est . . . Parteniacensi indulta, ut dictum est, venia, castra movet et in Blazonensem Theobaudum. . . ." *Ibid.*, p. 265. ". . . 1129: Fulcho comes pergit; et Gaufridus filius eius, honore adepto, ad Parteniacum exercitum duxit. . . ." *Chroniques des églises d'Anjou*, p. 33.

[72] In 1151 William II of Parthenay attended an assembly of Louis VIII at St. Hilaire-sur-l'Autize just south of the Gâtine. *Cartulaires de l'Absie*, pp. 87–88.

[73] *Gesta Henrici*. William Stubbs, ed., Rolls Series (London, 1867, I), 47.

the opposition and re-established his authority, but William III's
role in the uprising as well as his fate afterward are uncertain.
Yet if Henry himself failed to punish the Lord of Parthenay
then that task was carried out effectively in the following two
decades by his son and heir, Richard. Richard had been pardoned
by his father for being one of the ringleaders of the revolt and
to prevent any such further outbreaks, Henry II assigned him to
administer the duchy of Aquitane. A warrior unexcelled in com-
bat, Richard the Lionhearted waged unrelenting war against his
foes until at one time or another during the next twenty-five
years he had subdued at least temporarily nearly every baronial
line in southwestern France. Few of the particulars are known,
but it was probably after supporting an uprising in 1188 that
Hugh of Parthenay who succeeded his father William III was
brought to terms and paid heavily for his disloyalty by surrendering
his castle of Secondigny and possibly that of Hérisson to Count
Richard.[74]

At approximately the same time came a promise of relief from
another quarter. In 1180 Louis VII of France died and was
succeeded by his fifteen-year-old son, Philip II, who turned out
to be an ambitious, capable king concerned above all else with
aggrandizing the monarchy by enlarging the royal demesne. Basic
to his plan was the ejection of the English from their fiefs in
western France, and from the beginning of his reign Philip II
unceasingly encouraged the nobility in Normandy and Aquitaine
to conspire against their feudal suzerain, the king of England.
Thus with the two sovereigns quarreling with one another and
with each vying for the services of the nobility, the latter found
themselves in an ideal bargaining position. When Philip II accel-
erated his offensive in Aquitaine after the death of Richard the
Lionhearted in 1199, the new English king, John I, was forced
to make concessions to retain the loyalty of his great vassals. It
was doubtless under these circumstances that Hugh I recovered his
castle of Secondigny and the good graces of King John in 1202.[75]

---

[74] A Letter Patent of 1202 of which the full text is given below (footnote 75)
reveals that Richard had at one time taken Secondigny from Hugh of Parthenay by
force. See also p. 66, footnote 81.

[75] " Homines de Parthenay habent litteras domini regis patentes de simplici
protectione.

   Rex, etc., Hugone Archiepiscopo salutem. Mandamus vobis quod Segundin quod
Rex Richardus, frater noster, vobis efforciavit et reddidit Radulfo de Tannay firmetis

For the next half century the continuing rivalry between the English and French kings proved to be a reprieve for the lords of Parthenay as for so many other barons of Aquitaine who remained relatively independent by switching their allegiances back and forth from one side to the other. But the advance of Philip II and then later of Louis IX was inexorable, and after a series of defeats Henry III of England formally renounced in the treaty of Paris in 1259 his claims over much of western France, including Poitou.[76] With the Count of Poitou, henceforth directly responsible to the French king, now firmly in control of an increasingly powerful governmental machinery, the age of the independent barony of Parthenay formally came to an end.

The vicissitudes of the family of Parthenay in provincial politics in the last three-quarters of the twelfth century find no parallel in the internal history of their barony where their authority was unquestioned. Perhaps three-quarters of all the references to the lords of Parthenay from 1122–1200 are contained in charters of donation to the various monasteries of the region in which the donor states that he made his grant to the abbot in the presence of, or in the hand of the head of that family.[77] In other words the consent of the overlord of that land was required before it could be given to a religious establishment. With the aid of many such references it is possible to trace with a fair amount of accuracy the boundaries of the barony of Parthenay at the end of the twelfth century.[78]

et efforciatis et nos vobis erimus auxiliatores et defensores et vobis mandamus quod inde non placitabitis quamdiu dominus erimus nisi per voluntatum vostrum. T. me ipso apud Arches, 18 die Maii (1202)." *Rotuli Litterarum Patentium.* T. Duffus Hardy, ed., Record Commission (London, 1835, I), 11.

". . . Rex, etc., Hugoni Archiepiscopo, etc. Sciatis quod vos diligimus et diligemus sicut illum de quo ad plenum confidimus et sicut illum cuius antecessores antecessoribus nostris bene servierunt, et dampna vobis illata moleste fecimus scilicet operam adhibebimus diligentem, quod inde vobis satisfiat, et vobis consilium et auxilium conferemus ad castrum vostrum firmandum de Parthenay et efforciendum et omnibus aliis negociis vostris vos permovebimus, sicut dilectum et fidelem nostrum et sicut illum de quo confidemus. T. me ipso apud Belencunber 17 die mai. . . ." *Ibid.*

[76] Sir Maurice Powicke, *The Thirteenth Century, 1216–1307.* Oxford History of England (Oxford, 1953), pp. 126–27.

[77] A typical example is as follows: ". . . Petrus de la Reata dedit quicquid in borderia terrae . . . apud Parteniacum in platea, in presencia et in manu Guillelmi archiepiscopi. . . ." *Cartulaires de l'Absie,* p. 98.

[78] See map No. 3, p. 67.

These boundaries corresponded with the limits of the castellanies of Parthenay, Secondigny, and Champdeniers, the three
principal fortifications of the lord of Parthenay. In the northern
Gâtine the jurisdiction of the lord of Parthenay was bounded by
that of the viscount of Thouars and various of his vassals. The
domains of the lord of Chantemerle, a village perched on the
western edge of the region four miles northwest of l'Absie, occupied the corner of the Gâtine just north of that monastery.[79] To
the east, the southern extremity of the castellany of the Beaumonts,
lords of Bressuire and powerful vassals of the viscount of Thouars,
was contiguous with land of the lord of Parthenay just south of
the village and parish of Pugny.[80] Continuing to the east the
boundary passed above the castle of Hérisson which almost certainly belonged to the lord of Parthenay late in the eleventh
century, but which, late in the twelfth century, was in the possession of Thibaut Chabot, then the seneschal of the Count of
Poitou.[81] From Hérisson the northern border of the barony passed
eastward to include the fief of Gourgé and then bent to the north
to circumscribe the villages of Aubigny and Lamairé.[82] At Villeneuve and Assais just beyond Lamairé the lands of the lord of
Parthenay were confronted by those of the lords of Airvault—
around 1140 a brother of the viscount of Thouars held the title—
and Moncontours.[83] The farthest eastern limit of the barony was
reached at Thénezay where the lord of Parthenay's jurisdiction
ran up against that of the castellan of Mirebeau.[84] Since the lords
of Moncontours and Mirebeau were both important vassals of
the count of Anjou, the latter thus had direct access to Parthenay
lands through their common frontier from Villeneuve to Thénezay,
a fact which certainly helps explain why those two powers were
allies so frequently during the eleventh and twelfth centuries.

[79] *Cartulaires de l'Absie*, pp. 16, 79–80, 109–10.

[80] *Ibid.*, pp. 52, 95. *Chartes de Nouaillé*, p. 253. *Chartularium Sancti Jovini*,
pp. 22–24. Archives de Maine-et-Loire, Série 101H225, Nos. 35, 124, 789.

[81] One may speculate that after the baronial rebellion of 1188 Richard the Lionhearted took Hérisson as well as Secondigny away from the lord of Parthenay and
gave the former to Thibaut Chabot, one of his favored followers. *Cartulaires de
l'Absie*, p. 147.

[82] *Ibid.*, pp. 20, 55–56, 110. Archives de la Haute-Loire, 1H185, Nos. 2, 3.

[83] *Cartulaires de l'Absie*, pp. 101, 112, 113; Nos. 381, 391, 411, 434, 441. MSS
Dom Fonteneau, XXVI, 170.

[84] Bibliothèque Nationale, *Collection Gaignières*, F. L. 5480, p. 133. Archives de
Maine-et-Loire, Série 101H225 bis, No. 140b. *Extrait de Bourgueil*, p. 176.

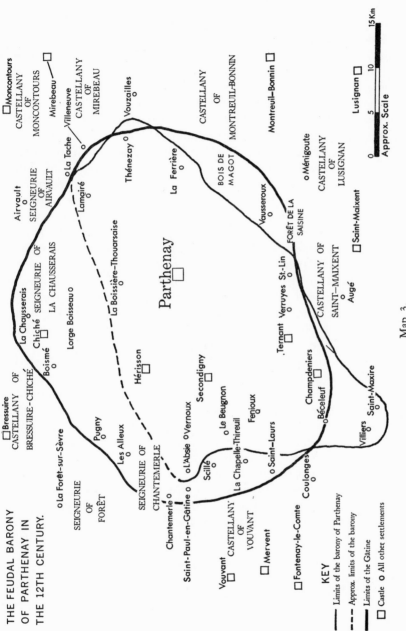

Map 3.

From Thénezay the eastern border turned sharply to the southwest to include la Ferrière and pass around the bois de Magot and the fôret de Vasles, two large forests which belonged to the count of Poitou and were part of his castellany of Montreuil-Bonnin eleven miles to the east.[85]

The southern boundary of the barony was formed where lands under the control of the lords of Parthenay met the castellanies of the lords of Lusignan and the monastery of St. Maixent. Circling the fôret de la Saisine, which belonged in part to the lords of Lusignan and Montreuil-Bonnin, it passed south to St. Lin, Verruyes, St. Remy, and Champeaux, after which it dropped below Champdeniers.[86] In the southwest Parthenay lands were hemmed in by the castellanies of Mervent and Vouvant, two fortresses under the control of the count of Poitou. From Champdeniers the line of demarcation turned north to pass between Fenioux, which was a fief of Parthenay, and St. Laurs belonging to the count.[87] It continued in the same direction through la Barre close by la Chapelle Thireuil which was the fief of a trusted vassal of the count.[88] Excluding Scillé, the boundary made a loop to the west to encircle the monastery of l'Absie-en-Gâtine which was in the territory of the lord of Parthenay.[89]

The political history of the Gâtine in the eleventh and twelfth centuries parallels that of scores of other regions of France at that time. At a time of chronically weak provincial government, a noble family gradually asserted almost complete independence of the territorial prince in the rule of the peoples on its lands and in the conduct of its external affairs, before succumbing to a greatly strengthened monarchy in the thirteenth century. Such in broad outline was the history of the Parthenays of the Gâtine who must be classed with the most powerful and renowned castellans, or middle-ranking nobility, in Poitou, and who contributed in good measure to the reputation of the Aquitainian nobility as one of the most unruly and uncontrollable in eleventh and twelfth

[85] *Cartulaire de Cormery*, pp. 90–93. *Cartulaire de St. Cyprien*, p. 280. *Cartulaire de Saint-Croix de Poitiers* (Revue Mabillon, IX), 74–75.

[86] Alfred Richard (ed.), *Archives du chateau de la Barre* (St. Maixent, 1868, II), 151. *Chartes de St. Maixent*, I, 120–21, 210–11, 213–14, 246–47, 272–73. *Cartulaires de l'Absie*, No. 24.

[87] *Chartes Poitevines de St. Florent de Saumurs*, p. 83.

[88] *Cartulaires de l'Absie*, p. 20. Archives d'Indre-et-Ioire, Série H24, No. 3.

[89] *Cartulaires de l'Absie*, p. 20. Archives d'Indre-et-Ioire, Série H24, No. 3.

century France. The material basis for this power came from wealth in revenues and one of the largest landed *seigneuries* in Poitou.[90] Small to begin with, its location in a largely uncleared, thinly populated region like the Gâtine offered the early lords of Parthenay opportunities for expansion which they exploited to the full with the construction of several new castles. Nor did they fail to profit from the new economic development of the eleventh century. The establishment of at least six new burgs in and around Parthenay with special privileges for their inhabitants stimulated a local cloth industry and attracted to the Gâtine some of the trade then beginning to pass along French roads. Moreover, having most of their lands concentrated in one continuous block rather than scattered, added to the strength of their position as did the strategically vital location of those lands. Since the Gâtine bordered on both Poitevin and Angevin lands and afforded a southerly approach through Poitou to the Saintonge, both counts were anxious to secure the loyalty of its lords as the several wars involving all three demonstrate. And especially the count of Poitou, for he had important estates on the eastern and western edges of the Gâtine which a hostile lord of Parthenay could seriously endanger. Most of the heads of the family used this location with considerable astuteness, threading their way in and out of the numerous wars of the two counts without serious damage to themselves. At the same time their loyalty to both sides gained them many favors in the form of domains in Bas-Poitou and the Saintonge, and high ecclesiastical offices for other members of their family.

The decline of the family of Parthenay occurred as a result of movements beyond its control. The consolidation of other castellanies on the borders of the Gâtine blocked further expansion after the barony had reached its greatest territorial extent in the early twelfth century. Then the growth of comital government and the transformation of Poitou into one of the principal battlegrounds of the French and English kings after 1180 exerted new pressures on the baronial houses of the provinces. Lack of a quick

[90] According to Jacques Boussard the largest *seigneuries* in western France in the twelfth century almost never exceeded fifty kilometers around the principal castle. The *seigneurie* of Parthenay measured fifty kilometers in the east-west and thirty-five kilometers in the north-south direction in the twelfth century. J. Boussard, *Le gouvernement d'Henri II Plantagenêt*, pp. 229–31.

and decisive outcome in the war enabled the family to switch its allegiance from one side to the other and thus to ward off the inevitable for several decades, but the inexorable advance of the French monarchy finally ended the days of the independent barony of Parthenay in the middle of the thirteenth century.

CHAPTER III

THE NOBILITY AND FEUDALISM

The rise of independent castellanies and, pre-eminently, that of the lords of Parthenay, radically transformed the political organization of the Gâtine in the eleventh and twelfth centuries. In the face of widespread insecurity resulting from the aftermath of the Norse invasions and from private wars only partially controlled by the count, the landowners of the Gâtine sought refuge at the hands of the castellans, who, in command of invulnerable stone castles, possessed the firmest base of political power in the region. Protection could be obtained, however, only at the price of personal subjection, and within a brief century nearly everyone in the Gâtine had commended himself either to the lord of Parthenay or to one of the castellans on the border of the region. It was through these relationships of dependence that the lords of Parthenay established their personal government over the region. Such relationships were not the same for everybody, however, but weighed much more heavily on the agricultural class than on the aristocracy and thus tended to accentuate the differences already existing between the two. The nature of these relationships in so far as they involved the nobility (in which case they were called feudal) is the subject to be treated next, with the latter part of the chapter being devoted to a general discussion of the noble class itself.

Since written documents almost never recorded such an event the only evidence for commendation to castellans in the Gâtine is of an indirect nature. Yet the more or less regular appearance of an individual at assemblies called by a castellan almost certainly indicates that he has become the vassal or follower of the latter. Although it is impossible to follow the development step by step, abundant charters by the year 1100 show that the lords of Parthenay had thus established their authority over the important landholders around their three major castles of Secondigny, Champdeniers, and Parthenay. In the vicinity of Secondigny it was the lords of Vernoux and Fenioux as well as a number of lesser men around the monastery of l'Absie who had become dependent on the lord of Parthenay.[1] Sometime before 1092 Geoffrey of Champdeniers had become the vassal of Ebbo and Gelduin of Parthenay who in 1093 also numbered among their dependents Gervais of Verruyes whose ancestor Simon had been one of the most powerful men in the Gâtine around 1040.[2] In the same manner they brought under their domination the leading families from around Parthenay including the lords of la Ferrière, Aubigny, la Peyratte, Lamairé, and Gourgé.[3]

People living in the outlying parts of the Gâtine commended themselves to one or the other of the several castellans located just outside the circumference of the region. In the north the castellans of Bressuire, Chiché, and la Chausserais, and in the south the lords of Vouvant and Montreuil-Bonnin claimed men of the Gâtine as their dependents.[4] Although none of these men alone came to command more than an isolated corner of the Gâtine, collectively they prevented the lord of Parthenay from making all of that country his own.

Precisely what was involved in the commendation of one man to another defies close analysis. Nevertheless one may arrive at a few safe generalizations about it by combining the few scraps of information which survive with what is known by modern scholarship in a broader European context.[5] The agreement between the two was concluded when one man paid homage to his lord, *dominus* or *senior*; that is, he became the man, *homo*, of his lord by kneeling and placing his hands in those of the

[1] *Cartulaire de St. Nicolas de Poitiers*, p. 83; *Cartulaires de l'Absie*, pp. 2, 5, 6, 9, 10, 18, 19, 20; Besly, *Histoire*, p. 396.

[2] Besly, *Histoire*, p. 396; *Chartes de St. Maixent*, I, 210, 211.

[3] *Cartulaire de Talmond*, pp. 163–77, 294; *Cartulaires de l'Absie*, p. 20; Bibliothèque Nationale, Gaignières, F. L. 17127, p. 379; Archives de la Haute-Loire, Série 1H185, Nos. 2 and 3.

[4] For references see the footnotes for pages 66 and 68 above.

[5] Bloch, *La société féodale*, I, 223–70. The study of feudal practices in Poitou by Paulette Portejoie, *Le régime des fiefs d'après la coutume de Poitou* (Poitiers, 1942), deals mainly with the thirteenth and fourteenth centuries.

latter.[6] He thus acknowledged at one and the same time his personal dependence on his lord and if there were any other obligations created by his act of homage, he agreed to carry them out. Following this, the vassal promised on oath to serve his lord faithfully, an action which lent a Christian overtone to an otherwise secular ceremony.

Occasionally the relationship between lord and man may have been purely personal, but in most cases it seems clear that it involved a fief as well. In return for certain services the lord bestowed upon his vassal a fief (in Latin *feudum* or *fevum*) or a source of income which might take the form of land, money, or produce and which was a tenure held only under certain conditions in contrast to an allod or property owned outright.[7] The offering of fiefs was most likely the principal method by which castellans persuaded men to become their vassals short of using intimidation or brute force. For in the society of the eleventh and twelfth centuries one index to a nobleman's prestige was the number of vassals he had and also how distinguished they were. The search for prominent followers led the lords of Parthenay well beyond the confines of their native Gâtine and sometimes resulted in their giving fiefs to men who were at least their equals in wealth and power. Giraud Berlais, the lord of Montreuil-Bellay in northern Poitou and one of the most powerful vassals of the count of Anjou held lands near le Beugnon southwest of l'Absie and seems to have been a vassal of the lord of Parthenay.[8] Other well-known Poitevin nobility who were vassals of the lord of Parthenay for fiefs in the Gâtine were the lords of Vaucouleurs north of Bressuire, who were also leading adherents of the viscount of Thouars, the Lobeth's of St. Maixent, and the lords of Tonnay-

---

[6] ". . . Ut autem Radulfus abbati tanquam domino suo et monachis suis honeste et fideliter obediret, abbas quoque eum sicut hominem suum (teneret), secundum conditiones que ibi facte sunt, factus est Radulfus abbatis homo junctis manibus." *Cartulaire de Talmond*, pp. 176–77.

[7] Fiefs in the Gâtine were usually grants of land which varied from small peasant exploitations to half a parish in size. *Cartulaires de l'Absie*, pp. 19, 112. *Extrait de Bourgueil*, pp. 115–16. On the other hand they could also be payments of money or of agricultural produce. For example Peter of Fontenioux near Parthenay held part of the proceeds of a mill in fief, whereas Giraud of le Theil in the same neighborhood received as a fief part of the tithe collected on all cows and sheep in the granges of Ecoussais and le Fouilloux on the northeastern edge of the Gâtine. *Cartulaires de l'Absie*, pp. 69, 91.

[8] *Ibid.*, pp. 22, 27, 88. Archives de la Haute-Loire, Série 1H185, No. 2.

Boutonne in the Saintonge, who were, to be sure, descended from a younger branch of the Parthenay line.[9]

Some of the vassals of the lord of Parthenay were wealthy enough to give fiefs to men of their own, thus creating another rank in the feudal hierarchy of the Gâtine. Foremost among them were the nobles who had custody of his castles in the region and who had to have knights of their own for purposes of defense. The lord of Verruyes had a number of vassals among whom the most noteworthy was Guy of Ternant, a powerful knight of the southeastern Gâtine around the year 1100.[10] Likewise, Boers of Champdeniers had his own knights and so did Geoffrey Fulchard of Secondigny castle.[11] Below the castellans were a few nobility who, even though they did not command castles, were still influential enough to keep their own armed vassals. Ralph Malclavel of Parthenay who had domains in nearly every part of the Gâtine numbered among his men a knight named Urias to whom he had given in fief some of the tithe in the parish of la Peyratte.[12] At least two other seigneurs from near Parthenay, Gilbert Meschin and Audeard Roux, also had knightly vassals.[13] Nevertheless, the examples of such subinfeudation are the exception rather than the rule, and the vast majority of men in possession of fiefs in the Gâtine seem to have held them directly from one of the castellans of the region.

A note of complication was struck, however, toward the middle of the twelfth century when the Benedictine monastery of St. Maixent just south of the Gâtine began to play an important role in the feudal affairs of that region. Throughout the century the abbots of that monastery received homage from most of the outstanding nobility in the vicinity, including among others the lords of Lusignan, the Chabots, lords of St. Hermine and Vouvant in the Vendée, and the viscounts of Aunay. Then they claimed the lords of Parthenay and Allonne as vassals for the fiefs of Beaulieu, Cour, Vouhé, la Boissière-en-Gâtine, Soutiers, and Allonne, all

---

[9] *Chartes Poitevines de St. Florent de Saumurs*, p. 83. *Cartulaires du Bas-Poitou*, p. 12. *Chartes de Nouaillé*, p. 253. Bibliothèque Nationale, Gaignières, F. L. 17127, p. 379. *Documents inédits* (Mémoires de la société de statistique des Deux-Sèvres, 1875), p. 285. Archives de Maine-et-Loire, Série 187H1, No. 1.

[10] *Chartes de St. Maixent*, I, 213, 241, 288.

[11] *Cartulaires de l'Absie*, pp. 2–8.

[12] *Cartulaire de Talmond*, p. 175.

[13] *Ibid.*, pp. 164, 166, 176.

villages in the southeastern Gâtine. And were it not for the loss of so many twelfth-century documents from the cartularies of the abbey, one would probably find that many of the villages of that part of the region were fiefs of St. Maixent, as indeed, they were in 1265.[14] There are several explanations for the prominence of the abbey in the feudal hierarchy of the Gâtine at that time. Founded in the latter years of the fifth century, St. Maixent was one of the most venerable monasteries in all France and prior to the Norse invasions had been one of the richest landowners in Poitou.[15] It is quite possible that the payment of homage by William III of Parthenay, and others, was tantamount to an acknowledgment that the fiefs in question were originally part of the enormous patrimony of the abbey before they had been alienated during the late Carolingian times.[16] On the other hand it is conceivable that by persuading them to become his vassals the abbot hoped to control in some measure the neighboring feudal lords who, through their private wars, were wreaking havoc on the abbey and its possessions. Whatever motives may have caused the lord of Parthenay to become a vassal of St. Maixent—and the desire for prestige, and respect for such an ancient and holy institution must not be ruled out—he certainly was aware that the abbot was far less able to coerce his men than was the count. By recognizing the abbot as his overlord for those fiefs instead of the count, he was further avoiding the grasp of the latter.

As it passed into common usage in the twelfth century, the kind of service owed by any fief tended to become more or less standard. Thus when Reginald, lord of Allonne, made a gift of land to the monastery of l'Absie around 1150, he promised to render the horse and court service and in general " all other things which are due from a fief " as if the latter were so well known that mention of them was unnecessary.[17] By mentioning the service of a horse, *equo servitii*, he placed emphasis on what was in most cases the primary obligation of a vassal to the lord from whom he held his fief—to furnish military assistance in one form or another. In an age when public government had practically

---

[14] *Chartes de St. Maixent*, I, 351–52, 358–59; II, 94.
[15] *Ibid.*, Introduction of Alfred Richard, p. XXXVIII.
[16] *Ibid.*, p. XLII.
[17] " . . . et concessit illam garire de plaisto et de equo servitii et de omnibus illis quae ad feodum pertinent." *Cartulaires de l'Absie*, p. 88.

disappeared and was replaced by the private jurisdictions of numerous independent castellans, force was the only means by which the latter could impose and maintain their authority. Furthermore, to survive the baronial wars which were commonplace in the eleventh and twelfth centuries, a private army was indispensable. The nature of the military service required and its duration are subjects about which the sources are obscure, yet it probably varied according to the size of the fief and the resources of its holder. In the case mentioned above, Reginald of Allonne had only to furnish a horse each year and avoided personal service.[18] Yet the fact that many of the most important vassals of the lord of Parthenay had houses in that castle suggests that they expected to perform some sort of castle guard duty over extended periods of time.[19] And surely it was those men who formed the cream of his army in time of war.

In addition to giving military assistance a vassal also had the privilege and duty of advising his lord in the making of decisions which concerned the interests of both of them. Thus when the lords of Vernoux set out to fix a standard size for the hedges in their lands, they did so only with the advice and consent of their men.[20] Deliberating about how he might make a gift to the monastery of l'Absie, Boers, the lord of Champdeniers, finally decided, with the approval of his wife, his friends, and his men, to give the monks a wine press in the castle.[21]

Whenever a lord summoned his vassals to advise him on some point, it happened almost as a matter of course that he took the opportunity to settle any disputes which may have arisen among them. Consequently an important part of a vassal's service in court was that of acting as a judge in cases involving his fellows. From a number of illustrations one may cite a controversy from the end of the eleventh century when a rear-vassal of the lord of Parthenay named Urias, threatened to take by force a revenue of some grain which he asserted was owed him by the priory of la

[18] This kind of substitution as well as the commutation of military service into payments of money was not uncommon in medieval Poitou. F. L. Ganshof, *Feudalism,* trans. Philip Grierson (2nd English ed., New York, 1961), p. 91.

[19] See below, pp. 90–91.

[20] ". . . has iidem Willelmus de Vernol et Gaufridus, consensu tam suorum quam Absiensium, taliter determinaverunt ut. . . ." *Cartulaires de l'Absie,* p. 78.

[21] ". . . Consilio itaque maritae meae et hominum meorum et amicorum, donavi. . . ." *Ibid.,* p. 5.

Peyratte, but which had not yet been paid. When the priory of la Peyratte contested his claims, the quarrel was taken before " the *curia* of Lord Ebbo (of Parthenay) and all his princes " who decided that the burden of proof lay with the prior.[22]

There were also times when a lord was served in court by his vassals for purely social reasons. In the feudal society of the eleventh and twelfth centuries, there was no more tangible demonstration of a man's prowess and distinction than an assembly where he was attended by a lengthy retinue of eminent vassals. A long list of vassals and servants accompanied Archbishop Joscelin and the Bishop of Poitiers at the donation of the burg of Secondigny to the abbey of Bougueil around 1070, a situation which repeated itself on many other occasions.[23]

Whether or not custom obligated the vassal in this period to assist his lord financially with the feudal aids is, although probable, uncertain due to the silence of the sources.[24] However, it did require him to pay a " relief " for the privilege of inheriting his father's fief. Relief, called variously *placitum de mortua manu*, *relevamine*, *relevamentum*, and *relevatio*, was a survival from the earliest days of infeudation when fiefs were granted for a lifetime only and when a payment had to be made in order for a son to succeed his father as the holder of his fief.[25]

The fief is normally thought of as an institution of the aristocracy because it required services such as fighting and court duty which could be performed only by someone possessed of considerable wealth and leisure. However, it would be an oversimplification to state that only nobles had fiefs. In an age when everyone, from the most indigent peasant to the strongest castellan, was bound to a lord and rendered certain services to him, it was perfectly natural that repayment in the form of a fief should spread through all levels of society. Thus people could describe as fiefs the land

---

[22] ". . . ad curiam domini Ebonis et omnium procerum ejus. . . ." *Cartulaire de Talmond*, p. 172.

[23] Bibliothèque Nationale, Gaignières, F. L. 17127, p. 379.

[24] To be sure the taxes exacted in a number of cases for the marriage of the lord's eldest daughter and for his ransom, if necessary, resemble the traditional feudal aids, and indeed were called feudal. But the fact that they were also called tallages suggests that they affected peasants and not nobility. See below, p. 112.

[25] ". . . aut propter relevationem domini morientis. . . ." *Cartulaire de Talmond*, p. 172. The numerous references to relief after the year 1100 indicate that by this time the heredity of fiefs had become an established principle of feudal tenure in the Gâtine.

and revenues given for the maintenance of a parish priest as well as the remuneration paid to a forester for his work.[26] And the fiefs which were held in return for the payment of some grain, or a few chickens, or rent in money, were in all probability the possessions of peasants.[27] Indeed a substantial number of the fiefs in the Gâtine in this period seem to fall into this category. But this in no way detracts from the fact that fiefs also formed the fundamental link between the lord of Parthenay and the nobility of the Gâtine and that the feudal relationship was the means by which the former attempted to govern his lands.[28]

How effective was the feudal relationship as a means of government? Were the feudal bonds which attached many vassals to the lord of Parthenay strong enough for him to regulate their activities and punish their misdemeanors? Among the highest ranks of the Poitevin nobility where feudal bonds united the count and his castellans, they were decidedly ineffectual. During the two centuries covered by this study the lords of Parthenay largely escaped the control of the counts.[29] Relations between the lords of Parthenay and their leading vassals in the Gâtine were not nearly so chaotic, however. The former made concerted efforts to discourage rebellion among their vassals which seem to have borne fruit. None of their men, except Simon of Verruyes, owned castles, and the latter had built his before becoming a vassal of Ebbo and Gelduin of Parthenay. Furthermore, by refusing to allow any single family to become hereditary castellans of either Secondigny or Champdeniers they kept a firm hold on those two castles. There is only one recorded instance of internal revolt in the Gâtine, and that was suppressed with a promptitude and energy which frightened the monk who described it. At the death of Geoffrey Gilbert, lord of Lamairé, around 1150, his nephews

---

[26] *Chartes de St. Maixent*, I, 120, 213.

[27] Archives de Maine-et-Loire, Série 231H1, No. 3. *Cartulaires de l'Absie*, p. 19.

[28] The importance to the lord of Parthenay of the services obtained from these fiefs is apparent in an act of 1169 in which William III granted the monks of l'Absie permission to acquire whatever pious donations they could in any of his fiefs so long as he did not thereby lose any service due him. That, he warned the monks in advance, he would not tolerate. ". . . dono eisdem et concedo in elemosinam omnes terras et talleas earum et quicquid juris mei est in eis quas habitatores Absiae acquisierant vel acquisituri sunt in cunctis feodis meis, excepto quod si, propter acquisitionem terrarum amodo acquirendarum alicujus feodati mei servitia amiserem, abbas Absiae inde miserationem meam expostulet." *Cartulaires de l'Absie*, p. 81.

[29] See above, Chapter II.

Brient and Chabot the younger, the sons of William Chabot, lord of Aubigny, claimed to be his rightful heirs. For some unknown reason William III of Parthenay would have none of it, and, chasing them out of the Gâtine, gave Lamairé to another of his knights.[30] The case of Guy of Vaucouleurs, lord of Fenioux, is also highly illustrative of the coercive powers wielded on occasion by the lords of Parthenay over their vassals. Guy felt the wrath of Ebbo of Parthenay when he attempted to donate his church to a monastery other than the one chosen by his lord. Harrassed and threatened with expulsion from his fief, Guy cancelled his original grant and gave the church of Fenioux to the priory of Parthenay-le-Vieux as requested.[31]

The superiority of the lord of Parthenay is also shown in his ability to make them accept judgments handed down by his feudal court. During the 1130's when a certain Simon was lord of Vernoux, one of his men gave some land to the monastery of l'Absie, but seven years later the new seigneur of Vernoux, Giraud, also the lord of Gourgé, contested the monks' right to the land. When they received no satisfaction from him they appealed to the lord of Parthenay who was the *advocatus* or defender of the monastery. William III came to Vernoux with his knights, heard the case, and then told Giraud to withdraw his claims which the

---

[30] ". . . post mortem Gausfridi Gilberti nobilissimi viri, cujus anima Christo donante requiescat in pace, nepotes ipsius, Briencius videlicet Chabot et alii qui heredes ejus fieri debuissent, extra Gastinam exules sunt ejecti malivolencia et persecutione Willelmi cognomento Archiepiscopi. Tunc miles quidam, Bucardus nomine, filius Petri Droconis, honorem et possessionem memorati Gausfridi Gilberti dono et concessione Willelmi Archiepiscopi injuste rapuit et obtinuit. . . ." *Cartulaire de Talmond*, pp. 294–95.

[31] " Ego G. de Valde Colorata dictus, cum mei terram patrimonii, quae est apud Finiacum, a Parteniacensibus dominis recipissem, pro meis et mei patris delictis aecclesiam quae ibi erat Sancti Florentii monachis condonavi: Geldoino Parteniaci domino concedente, Guidone Sanctae Crucis canonico existente teste, et Petro Pictavensis episcopo se concessurum libenter promittente. In sequenti vero, dum domnus Ebo Veteris Partiniaci aecclesiam Sancti Rotberti Dei Casae monachis dedisset et de suis propriis nimium attribuisset, ut potens dominus, mihi suo homini precipit quatinus Finiaci aecclesiam Sancti Rotberti monachis faverem; quam Sancti Florentii monachis me donasse respondi. Qua de causa nimium mihi infestus et me expulsurum a patrimonio asserens nisi suae voluntate obedirem, constrictus sic ab Ebonis inimicia, et nolens eius frui tristicia, quod concedere poteram Sancti Rotberti monachis seculario concessi: me bene Petro, Sancti Rotberti monacho, dicente numquam sibi hoc donum supradictum Willelmus filius Simonis et Symon frater Willelmi et Radulfus filius Geldoini concesserunt." *Chartes poitevines de St. Florent près Saumur*, p. 83.

latter did straightway.[32] Another time one of the men of Ebbo the Gelduin of Parthenay, named Thibauld Garin, refused to accept his portion of the tithe of the parish of la Peyratte, asserting that the monks had changed measures and were weighing out less than they did formerly. Taken before the lords of Parthenay and " the entire *curia* of Parthenay," the monks were ordered to prove their point by oath and battle. Thibaud then forfeited the case when he announced that he would not accept the result, but he was forced to do so anyhow by the *curia*.[33]

These examples might lead one to believe that the domination of the lord of Parthenay over his vassals was quite secure, yet on the other hand there are just as many indications that the latter went their own ways without much interference from their superior. For one thing they appear to have engaged in private wars among themselves without fear of reprisal from their lord. Simon of Verruyes was the target of a papal censure in 1110 for molesting a priory of St. Maixent near Montreuil-Bonnin west of the Gâtine, and it may have been in a private feud that Guy of Ternant was taken prisoner in 1093, following which he extorted some ransom money from the monks of St. Maixent under the guise of charity.[34] Inured to a life of fighting, the nobles of the Gâtine could be ruthless and brutal, and on occasion they killed with impunity. Around 1112 the same Guy of Ternant murdered a monk of St. Maixent, but it was his conscience and not his feudal lord which caused him to repent, and even then the retribution which he paid for his crime was a mere token gift of land.[35] Reginald, lord of Allonne, seems to have been a particularly unsavory character who achieved notoriety at least twice for his violence. One time he killed a man from St. Pompain, south of the Gâtine, after which he repented to the extent of giving the

---

[32] ". . . Andreas Prevelerals et Manuels frater ejus, concedentibus filiis suis, dederunt S. Mariae et Petro abbati et monachis Absiae unam borderiam in terra sua in bosco; postea in tempore Willelmi abbatis Geraudus de Gorge donum supradictum calumpniavit quod libere in tempore Symonis de Vernol jam VII annis possederant. Quapropter Willelmus abbas et monachi clamorem facientes ad Archiepiscopum dominum Parteniaci in cujus defensione erat locus Absie, ad Vernol, hac de causa, cum militibus suis venit; qui audientes causam locuti sunt cum Giraudo ut calumniam quam injuste faciebat monachis dimitteret; qui statim dimisit et concessit . . .," *Cartulaires de l'Absie*, p. 20.

[33] *Cartulaire de Talmond*, p. 175.

[34] *Chartes de St. Maixent*, I, 213, 261.

[35] *Ibid.*, p. 288.

monastery some lands, both for the soul of the deceased and in order to have peace with his friends.[36] Then another time he arbitrarily hanged a man, and for this outrage he agreed to pay liege homage to the abbey of St. Maixent, plus a sum of seven pounds in Angevin money.[37] It is not perhaps worth noting that crimes of this kind were commonplace in the Gâtine in the eleventh and twelfth centuries, but it is significant that the lords of Parthenay either made no effort or were in no position to restrain or punish wayward vassals. Confession of guilt and agreement to pay some compensation appear to have been purely voluntary on the part of the latter.

The lords of Parthenay seem to have been equally disinterested in, or incapable of, interfering in many of the countless disputes which arose between their vassals and various churches over the possession of land and the collection of revenues. The early twelfth-century records for just two parishes in the eastern Gâtine, la Peyratte and Lamairé, bring to light an astounding number of disputes between those institutions and the petty landowners of the district. Nearly all of them started when someone contested the legitimacy of donations made to the church in the past, and seized the land or revenue—very often the tithe—in question. Once this happened the parish priest immediately protested and sought to have it restored. There were several ways in which the church gained its end, but once again it is interesting to discover that almost never was it through the threat of force.[38] The lord of Parthenay, who was conspicuously absent from most of these fracases, was indeed asked three different times to hear a case with his feudal court and decide after the medieval custom, how guilt was to be established.[39] However, the church got little satisfaction from him since in two instances he and his men judged that the burden of proof rested with it, and on the other occasion he engineered, after a great deal of controversy, a settlement which

[36] ". . . pro anima Petri Clerbaus quam interfecerat et pro pace amicorum ejus habenda . . .," *Cartulaires de l'Absie*, p. 88.

[37] ". . . Reginaldus d'Alona est homo legius abbati sancti Maxentii et placitum in voluntate ipsius abbatis, et ipse abbas P. Raimundus, pro eo quod in voluntate sua pendebat, accepit ab eo septem libras Andegavensis monete . . .," *Chartes de St. Maixent*, I, 358–59.

[38] Quite naturally only disputes with a successful outcome were written up. Consequently, the lost causes, which must have been numerous, escape the modern observer.

[39] *Cartulaire de Talmond*, pp. 172–76.

was a victory for neither side. Moreover, the prior of la Peyratte then had to pay Ebbo of Parthenay a fancy fee for the " protection " of his church, a fact which leaves a strong suspicion that the lord of Parthenay entered legal cases mainly for pecuniary reasons.

Just as happened in case of a murder, the vassals of the lord of Parthenay most often gave up their claims because of personal contrition and anxiety for the salvation of their souls.[40] And almost invariably the church had to pay a heavy price to win what were essentially Pyrrhic victories. For example, the prior of la Peyratte had long fulminated against a knight, Urias of Parthenay, because he had usurped one and one-half measures—*modera*—of grain from the tithe of the church of la Peyratte, and when he was finally persuaded to abandon his possession of it, Urias received no less than 340 shillings as a reward " for his charity." [41]

War, murder, uninhibited seizure of land and revenues, repentance induced by bribes; these do not create an impressive balance sheet in favor of law and order, and in fact, cast grave doubts on their very existence. And yet, on the other hand, the lords of Parthenay clearly demonstrated that, if they felt it necessary, they were strong enough to suppress their men. All of the above adds up to the fact that the feudal relationship had a very limited sphere of influence insofar as preservation of peace and order was concerned. Obedience to a feudal superior did not imply any restriction of a vassal's activities other than treasonous ones. The vassals of the lord of Parthenay were free to do as they pleased without fear of reprisal so long as they abstained from rebellion and performed the services due from their fiefs. The turbulence and brutality which characterize the eleventh and twelfth centuries were a direct result of the freedom enjoyed by each minor landlord to act as he wished, providing he did not injure his lord.

All men in the Gâtine were dependent in one way or another on the lord of Parthenay and his castellans, but a few stood out from the rest of society to form an elite class, the nobility. Except for the lord of Parthenay who was called *dominus* or seigneur, the lack of any titles to designate these men sometimes makes it

---

[40] " . . . . pro redemptione animae suae et suorum. . . ." Archives de Maine-et-Loire, Série 101H225 bis, No. 124.

[41] " . . . de caritate sua . . .," *Cartulaire de Talmond*, p. 175.

difficult to separate them from peasants or men of more modest standing.[42] Nonetheless, the documents make abundantly clear in many other ways that this small group was far and away the dominant force in the Gâtine, the force which controlled the destiny of the region and its peoples.

Mere chance has left some parts of the Gâtine well documented in contrast to the almost complete obscurity of others, especially the north, thus making it impossible to determine the exact size of the noble class. Nonetheless, all evidence suggests that it constituted an extremely small portion of the entire society. In an area of some forty parishes in the central and southern parts of the region, only eighteen families are well attested as being noble, with several others probable despite lack of unequivocal proof.[43] Such a figure refers only to the noble lines indigenous to the region excluding at least eight and probably many others who had estates in the Gâtine even though their main holdings were elsewhere.[44] Although their origins may have been, and probably were, earlier, most appeared first at the end of the eleventh or during the early part of the twelfth century with only four, headed by the family of Parthenay, known to have flourished prior to 1050. No clear pattern emerges from a glance at the

[42] The titles, *nobilissimi viri*, given to Geoffrey Gilbert of Lamairé around 1140 and *nobilis vir*, attributed to the lord of Parthenay in 1192 were entirely exceptional. *Cartulaire de Talmond*, p. 294. *Chartes de St. Maixent*, I, 381.

[43] In the following is the name of each family, its location, and the earliest reference to it. The lords of Parthenay, Besly, *Histoire*, p. 396, ca. 1010. The lords of la Chapelle Thireuil, *Chartes de St. Maixent*, I, 129, ca. 1040. The lords of Verruyes, *ibid.*, p. 120–21, ca. 1040. The Grosgrents, lords of Vernoux, *ibid.*, p. 140, 1049. The Malclavel's of Parthenay, la Peyratte, etc., Bibliothèque Nationale, Gaignières, F. L. 17127, p. 379, ca. 1070. The Fulchard's, lords of Secondigny, *ibid.*, ca. 1070. The Maingot's, lords of la Chausserais, *Chartes de St. Maixent*, I, 171, 1078. Gilbert Meschin of Parthenay, *Cartulaires du Bas-Poitou*, p. 93, 1078. The lords of Champdeniers, *Cartulaire de St. Cyprien*, p. 331, 1090. The lords of Ternant, *Chartes de St. Maixent*, I, 211, 1091. William Vivian of Secondigny, *ibid.*, p. 233, 1099. The Gilbert's of Lamairé and la Peyratte, *Cartulaire de Talmond*, p. 168, ca. 1100. The Chabot's of Lamairé and la Peyratte, *ibid.*, p. 164, ca. 1100. The Roux of Parthenay, Lamairé, and la Peyratte, *ibid.*, p. 136, ca. 1100. The lords of le Theil, *Cartulaires de l'Absie*, p. 50, ca. 1120. The Gerard's, lords of Chiché, Archives de Maine-et-Loire, Série 101H225, No. 789, 1126. The lords of Gourgé, *Cartulaires de l'Absie*, p. 11, ca. 1135. The lords of Allonne, *ibid.*, p. 2, ca. 1140. The lords of Billy, Archives de Maine-et-Loire, Série 101H225 bis, No. 396, 1154. Billy, La Chausserais, and Chiché are in the far northern part of the Gâtine where the documentation is thinnest.

[44] Notable among these were the lords of Talmond, Montreuil-Bellay, Bressuire, Chateaumur and Vaucouleurs.

geographical distribution of the class. With the exception of the two or three families whose principal residences were in Parthenay, the nobility was a rural class living in the hamlets of the region, as is evidenced by their tendency to name themselves after those villages.[45] They were not evenly spread over the region, for a number of well-documented villages and parishes like those around l'Absie seem to have had no nobility at all. On the other hand the parishes of Lamairé and la Peyratte contained at least four noble houses. Other nobility, of whom there is little or no record, undoubtedly lived in the northern Gâtine, but at the rate of roughly one family for two parishes probably only eight or ten more. In its reduced size the nobility in the Gâtine resembles its counterpart in the county of Namur more closely than that in the Maconnais where there was approximately one family per parish.[46] The obvious explanation for this phenomenon was the sparse population of the region.

The nobility of the Gâtine was, to begin with, an economic class and was distinguished from the peasantry by its extensive landed wealth. Only the vaguest generalizations can be made about the size and number of landholdings of any man, whether peasant or noble, in the eleventh and twelfth centuries, since the only surviving descriptions of such lands were those made by churchmen at the moment when laymen donated something to the church. Such descriptions are imprecise and necessarily incomplete since no one, unless dying without heirs, would give away everything he owned. Still they are sufficient to show that men suspected from other sources to be noble gave more land and more frequently than did peasants. The prodigality of Simon of Verruyes to the abbey of St. Maixent in 1040 provides a basis for a rough estimate of his total wealth. At that time Simon made a series of gifts to the abbot which included churches, revenues, and nine manses of land. It scarcely needs mentioning that a man who could afford to donate much property must have had many times that amount in reserve.[47] Large estates were of course indispensable to the nobleman since as the only significant source of wealth at that

[45] For instance the lords of Vernoux, Gourgé, Allonne, etc.

[46] Duby, *La société*, p. 411. Léopold Genicot, *L'économie rurale Namuroise au bas moyen âge*, Vol. 2, *Les hommes—La noblesse* (Recueil de travaux d'histoire et de philologie de l'Université de Louvain, 4th Series, 20th Fascicule), p. 14.

[47] *Chartes de St. Maixent*, I, 120–21.

time they alone enabled him to dress, arm, and lead the kind of life associated with his class.

A brief description of the possessions of the lord of Vernoux in the twelfth century will give an idea of the territorial basis for the power of a moderately important vassal of the lord of Parthenay. Near the castle of Secondigny, of which he was a knight, Simon of Vernoux had some woods in the land of les Braudières, whereas, further south adjoining the fief of Salmora he owned land at places called la Barre and les Vaux. To the west in the parish of St. Paul-en Gâtine, Giraud of Gourgé, who became lord of Vernoux after the death of his brother Simon around 1135, collected taxes on a manse of land from the fief of John St. Paul. The *domaines* of la Raimondière and la Vialière to the north and west of Vernoux also belonged to Giraud as did the land of Bonnefontaine to the northeast.[48] These lands which come to light only at the moment when they passed into the possession of the monastery of l'Absie, necessarily constituted just a minute portion of the entire *seigneurie*, but they show that it formed a rough circle centered on the village of Vernoux and extending in every direction from three to six miles.

Not all noblemen had their lands in one compact block as did the lord of Vernoux, but some like Ralph Malclavel, another vassal of the lord of Parthenay, had *domaines* in many parts of the region. At the middle of the eleventh century the earliest known member of this family was the dominant seigneur in the parish of la Peyratte along with Kadelo who became lord of Talmond in 1058. Shortly after 1100 a descendant of the same name had acquired *domaines* on the southern edge of the Gâtine at Béceleuf, Blaoer, Dislai, Fougère, and seems to have become lord of Fenioux. In addition to that, the Malclavel's had possessions in a ten-mile area bordering the northeastern Gâtine near Lamairé and probably were the founders of a new town, *Villanova*, five miles north of Thénezay. Finally the family collected some revenues in the land of Brèchepote near Faye-l'Abbesse in the northern Gâtine.[49] The size and extent of their *domaines* made the Malclavel's one of the first-ranking noble families of the region.

Not all noble lands were held in the same way. The conversion

---

[48] *Cartulaires de l'Absie*, pp. 10, 11, 19, 52, 55, 74, 88, 98, 99.

[49] *Ibid.*, pp. 1, 3, 57, 60, 61, 112. *Cartulaire de Talmond*, pp. 173–75. Archives de Maine-et-Loire, Série 101H225 bis, No. 192.

of private property into fiefs ultimately affected the estates of every great landholder in the region, but not to the extent of eliminating the former. On the contrary, many noblemen appear to have retained allods along with their fiefs, and whenever appropriate they distinguished between the two in their charters. Prior to 1050 the term *allodum* normally designated private property, but after that time it gave way to the word *proprium*, meaning literally "what one owned." It may be that *proprium* expressed more exactly and forcefully than allod the antithesis between a fief and fully-owned property. The ratio between the two kinds of land in the holdings of noblemen of the Gâtine is unknown, but the relative frequency of their donations without the approval of a superior, as would be necessary if the land in question was a fief, leaves the impression that the former had enough allodial land to be economically independent of their feudal lords.

As in the rest of medieval France noble estates included two different kinds of land, the reserve or *domaine*, maintained for the lord's immediate uses, and the tenures which peasants held from him on a hereditary basis. Even though the average size, and consequently the economic importance, of the reserve in relationship to the tenures on any estate cannot be determined, one can conclude that the latter were important sources of income furnishing both food and money.[50] Among the revenues deriving from the tenures the *terrage*, or a part of the harvest, and *complant*, its counterpart for vineyards, seem to have been more valuable than the *cens* or land rent. Despite the many gifts of all, or portions of, the tithe to neighboring monasteries, the vigor and persistence with which many nobles pursued claims to the right to that revenue indicate that it was highly valued.[51] Possession of the large woodlands of the region was turned to profit through charging peasants for pasturage rights for their livestock. In the same manner peasants and churchmen paid for the privilege of fishing in the many ponds and rivers which seem in most cases to have been the property of noblemen. Peasants also paid revenues for the use of the mills, ovens, and wine presses built and maintained by the nobility. Some lords also owned churches,

---

[50] The scattered references to domain land never mention size.
[51] See page 92 where one such contestation is discussed.

but the Gregorian reforms put an end to that by the beginning of the twelfth century.[52]

Separating them from the peasantry, possibly even further than the disparity in wealth, was the power of many of the nobility. In the absence of any public authority many nobles imposed on a helpless peasantry various protection and assistance taxes called customs, among which the most common were the *taille* and *commendize*. Whereas he collected the other taxes as a landlord the nobleman collected these in his capacity as a ruler, a capacity which lent considerable prestige as well as being financially remunerative. But perhaps nowhere else was the gulf between the two classes so keenly felt as in the ability of some noblemen to police the lands of their peasants and to apprehend, sentence, and punish any suspected of misdemeanors. The details of only two disputes between peasants and their seigneur have survived, but they are enough to give striking proof of the stern superiority of the latter. Around 1140 Geoffrey Gilbert, lord of Lamairé, heard in his court a case about some tithes in the *domaine* of Seneuil which the local prior claimed were being taken unjustly by some of Geoffrey's men. Deciding that the monk was right, Geoffrey ordered his men to desist, but they were reluctant to do so. Then in the presence of both parties, Geoffrey commanded his *prévôt* to gather the donkeys which were used to carry the tithe, and had some killed and the ears cut off others.[53] This incident, which may seem quaint and rather primitive, was, nonetheless, a strong warning to his men of the consequences of further transgressions. Whether all, or most, nobility had such judicial power and whether it extended to competence over anything more than property disputes is questionable, but the effect of that power on the status of those who possessed it is not.[54] And in any

---

[52] The monk of 1120 who wrote that a church near l'Absie had belonged to a lay seigneur in the previous century, then felt called upon to explain parenthetically that in those times there were lay churches, ". . . in tempore illo erant ecclesiae laicorum . . ." as if his readers would not otherwise understand the situation. *Cartulaires de l'Absie*, p. 7.

[53] ". . . unde conventi ab eodum monachi et postmodum a domino Gosfrido Gilberti, cum nollent acquiescere, Paganus ipsius prepositus Goffridi, eo jubente, presentibus ipsis, asinos decimam colligentes, alios occidit, aliorum auriculas gladio obtruncavit . . .," *Cartulaire de Talmond*, p. 293.

[54] The custom of *vicaria* which normally referred to the right of justice in this period is encountered occasionally in the Gâtine and it seems likely that the same right was comprehended by the broader and more common word *dominium*, but

event all noblemen, even if lacking such jurisdiction of their own, were immune to the various customs imposed on the *homines consuetudinarii*, or men subject to customs, as peasants were sometimes called. This alone was a distinction of considerable moment.

Another tangible demonstration of the power, as well as of the prestige, of the nobility of the Gâtine was their command over various followers of their own. It may be presumed that many, if not all, hired a group of minor officials to manage the business on their lands. The lords of Parthenay doubtless set the standard with a household of servants and officials which was in miniature a replica of the courts of more eminent personages such as the count of Poitou or the king of France himself. Standing out among a large, unnamed group of officials qualified as ministers, *ministri*, were estate managers, police officers and legal advisors.[55] It is doubtful, however, whether many nobles kept a personal chaplain as did William III in the twelfth century.[56] But most important of all, many nobles were accompanied by armed vassals or knights who served both as personal bodyguards and attendants at court.[57] What could have been a more convincing display of his power and authority over peasants than the appearance of the nobleman with his officials and knights, or what was in effect his own private army?

The nobility of the Gâtine also led a different kind of life than the peasantry. To be sure there was a certain similarity in that both were rural classes with the nobility housed on their estates in the country, side by side with their men. The parallel ends there, however, for the nobleman was an agricultural administrator instead of actually working the soil. For the cultivation of his own *domaines* he relied on his peasant tenants, and for the task of supervision, on the labor of the minor functionaries whom he enlisted from among his men. These same officials who aided in running his estates could also relieve their lord to devote a large portion of each year to military and other pursuits. Hunting

---

neither term is ever defined. The second example of a seigneurial count in action is recorded in the *Cartulaire de Talmond*, p. 295.

[55] On these officials, see below, pp. 117–19.

[56] *Cartulaires de l'Absie*, p. 82.

[57] The noble families about which the most is known, the Malclavel's, the Maingaud's, the Roux, the Gilbert's and Gilbert Meschin of Parthenay and la Peyratte, and the lords of Champdeniers and Verruyes all had knightly vassals. *Ibid.*, pp. 5–7. *Cartulaire de Talmond*, pp. 164–66, 174. *Chartes de St. Maixent*, I, 241.

was another activity which was an integral part of the noble's existence and one befitting a man of leisure. One of the principal reasons why many seigneurs carefully controlled the cutting of trees in their woods was doubtless to preserve them as game reserves.

In their religious life the nobility kept company mainly with the ecclesiastical aristocracy of the region, and the lord of Parthenay even had his own personal chaplain thus avoiding the ordinary parish church.[58] If they chose the church as a career, they settled for only the highest offices as, for example, William Gilbert of Parthenay who first became the archdeacon of Poitiers and then was elected bishop of the diocese of Poitou in 1117.[59] Their taste for war and violence led some seigneurs to commit acts of great brutality against religious institutions, even to the point of killing churchmen, but the life of most was characterized by at least a degree of piety which caused them to make bountiful gifts to churches. The foundation of a monastery or a church was always the occasion for the nobility to exhibit their chivalric largess. At the consecration of the Cistercian monastery at l'Absie in 1120, almost every noble and affluent peasant in the western Gâtine gave some land or revenues, and some gave several times. The construction of nearly all the parish churches in the Gâtine was the work of the aristocracy of the tenth and eleventh centuries, and until the Gregorian reforms after 1075, the same men appointed and paid the priest, and kept most of the ecclesiastical proceeds. Then whenever a man, whether peasant or noble, was dying he was automatically expected to make retribution for his sins by giving land to the church. Furthermore it was not uncommon for aged noblemen to shed their armor and put on the monastic habit in order to end their lives, and be buried, in a monastery.[60] In return for his generosity the nobleman was permitted to share in the spiritual benefits of the monastic congregation and often to have masses said for his soul after death. The stipulation of one man upon granting land to St. Maixent is rather touching: ". . . and therefore I gave [land] in order

[58] *Cartulaires de l'Absie*, p. 82.
[59] *Ibid.*, p. 8, footnote 1.
[60] Two successive generations of the ruling family of Ternant, Ermengod in 1098 and Ingelelme in 1111, made generous gifts to the abbot of St. Maixent in return for acceptance into the monastic congregation there. *Chartes de St. Maixent*, I, 230, 272, 273.

that every Sunday in church remembrance shall be made to the parish of me and all those who lie with me in the cemetery." [61]

It was far more efficacious for a nobleman to redeem past sins by making a pilgrimage at least once in his life to one of the holy places which were located all over medieval Europe. Since the Gâtine lay near a heavily traveled road leading to the basilica of St. James of Compostella in Spain, it was perfectly natural that the nobility should be drawn to that shrine, one of the most famous in western Europe. It was there that William II of Parthenay made a pilgrimage in 1169, no doubt accompanied by a large following of his vassals, and it appears that William, lord of Chantemerle was enroute to St. James when he died in Dax, south of Bordeaux, late in the twelfth century.[62] But nothing counted quite so much as participation in a crusade or holy war, an experience which must often have been the most exciting and novel in the entire life of many a noble. Ebbo of Parthenay almost certainly participated in the first crusade from 1096–99 in the company of his principal vassals, whereas other nobility of the Gâtine journeyed to the Holy Land for the second and third crusades in 1147 and 1189.[63] It is difficult to appreciate the profound impression which those long and strenuous journeys and the encounters with foreign cultures must have had on the provincial mentality of the nobility of a remote region like the Gâtine. Yet evidence is not entirely lacking, for in Parthenay alone three different churches owed their origins to crusades and pilgrimages, those of St. Croix, Saint Sépulchre, and St. Jacques.[64] By importing from Palestine a new style of architecture for the construction of the Church of the Holy Sepulchre, Ebbo of Parthenay opened his region to new influences from abroad, something which, one may be sure, happened in many other spheres than that of religious architecture.

The houses which a substantial number of nobles maintained in the castles of Parthenay, Secondigny, and Champdeniers testify to another characteristic noble activity, that of service to the lord

---

[61] ". . . et ideo dedi ut omni die dominico ad parrochiam fiat rememoratio mea in ecclesia pro me et omnibus qui ibidem in cimiterio mecum jacent." *Ibid.*, p. 329.

[62] *Cartulaires de l'Absie*, pp. 81, 109.

[63] See above, p. 57, footnote 51; *Cartulaire de Talmond*, pp. 170, 281, 282. *Cartulaires de l'Absie*, pp. 79, 80.

[64] Ledain, *La Gâtine*, p. 96.

of Parthenay and his castellans.[65] For a given period of time each year, or in cases of emergency when they were called on to help guard or defend the castle, they thus had a place of lodging. Then most nobles periodically attended their lord at social events such as banquets and weddings, and witnessed his charters at formal, solemn occasions such as the founding of new churches or monasteries. In addition to carrying out these duties they formed the feudal *curia* or court which met with him to give advice on matters of common interest and to settle disputes among themselves.[66] It would not be correct, however, to picture the ordinary nobleman as a man of great legal experience or knowledge, since he was never called upon to judge guilt or innocence in a case, but merely to decide which party the burden of proof rested upon and which method of proof was to be applied in settling the dispute. And, in fact, he seldom had to do that since most quarrels ended in a settlement or compromise long before there was any question of the judgment of God.

The reference to the military activities of the nobility focuses attention on a major problem for the historian of this period, namely, the identity of a group of men entitled knights, *milites*, who, although few in number, appeared frequently and prominently at that time. Stated briefly, the question is whether knights were the same as nobles; whether the term *miles* was simply another name for a nobleman, or whether a distinction existed between the two. And if so, what was the nature of the distinction? To be sure contemporary monastic writers were sometimes curiously imprecise in the use of the word *miles,* one time employing it and the next time not when describing the same man.[67] A partial explanation for this is that the term could have two different meanings, the first of which was simply any one, regardless of his origin or status, who was armed to fight on horseback.

[65] For nobility with houses in Parthenay castle, *Cartulaire de Talmond,* pp. 164, 170, 173, 177, 315. *Cartulaires de l'Absie,* pp. 89, 99. Archives de Maine-et-Loire, Série 101H225 bis, Nos. 192, 396; Champdeniers castle, *Cartulaires de l'Absie,* pp. 5–7; Secondigny castle, *Chartes de St. Maixent,* I, 233, 276. *Cartulaires de l'Absie,* pp. 5, 100.

[66] Several sessions of the *curia of* Ebbo and Gelduin of Parthenay are recorded in the cartulary of Talmond for the years around 1100. *Cartulaire de Talmond,* pp. 172–77. Another involving the monks of l'Absie in the *curia* of the lords of Parthenay is mentioned in their cartulary. *Cartulaires de l'Absie,* p. 20.

[67] Around the turn of the eleventh century Guy of Ternant twice received the title, but not a third occasion. *Chartes de St. Maixent,* I, 213, 241, 288.

That this was not its most common usage, however, is shown by the fact that with one exception none of the members of the nobility who were clearly thus equipped ever used the word before his name.[68]

Most of the time *miles*, in addition to the first meaning, seems to have been a title designating men who were dependent on, or vassals of, the nobility, a relationship often succinctly expressed by the notation that these men were the knights of the lord in question, *milites sui*.[69] The knight appears to have been a kind of armed servant or bodyguard who accompanied his lord, witnessed his charters, protected him, and carried out whatever tasks of a military nature he might require. For instance Rainier Faber, a knight of the Roux family of Parthenay and la Peyratte, represented, doubtless at the request of his lord, the monks of the priory of la Peyratte in a duel to decide a dispute about a tithe in that parish.[70] This same incident demonstrates in a dramatic fashion the degree to which at least one knight was dependent on his superiors. The *curia* of Ebbo and Gelduin of Parthenay ordained that the judgment of God in the form of a duel should be applied in order to prove which side was in the right. Each side chose a knightly pledge, *fidejussor*, to act in his stead and fight for him, but when the day for battle arrived Thibaud Garin, who was opposing the monks, announced that he would not accept such a judgment. The *curia* then decided that he had forfeited his claim and the prior of la Peyratte marched straightway to the house of Thibaud's pledge, Odo son of Jodoin, and stripped him of his lance and shield which he afterwards gave to his own pledge.[71] The meaning of this curious affair is clear enough: Odo had failed

---

[68] In a charter of around 1040 Symon of Verruyes made some gifts to the monastery of St. Maixent. Most of the charter is in the first person with Symon speaking and referring to himself simply by name, but at one point the monastic writer lapsed into the third person and described Symon as *miles Symon*. *Miles* in this case was not a title or else Symon himself would have taken it, but was just a term to identify him as a fighting man. *Ibid.*, p. 120–21.

[69] Thus when Gilbert Meschin witnessed a charter around 1100 he was attended by Baudouin his knight, ". . . vidente Gilbert Meschino et Baudino milite suo. . . ." *Cartulaire de Talmond*, p. 16.

[70] *Ibid.*, pp. 175–76.

[71] ". . . quapropter judicatum est illud esse revictum ab hac requisitione; unde mox supradictus monachus ivit in domum fidejussoris sui, scilicet Odonis Jodoini, et accepit inde scutum et lanceam et dedit famulo suo et portavit in domum Aldeardis Rufe. . . ." *Ibid.*

to carry out his obligations as pledge for Thibaud Garin—even though it was not his own doing—and had to pay by surrendering the weapons which he should have used in the duel and which made him a knight. To be treated in such a way in the presence of the greatest men of the region must have been a humiliating experience and have reminded Odo, in a most convincing way, of his subservience to his superiors.

The knights of the Gâtine were not insignificant people, however, but performed many of the same functions and lived in much the same way as the nobility. Thus on one occasion in the twelfth century the lord of Parthenay called upon his knights to judge a land dispute in the western Gâtine.[72] And most knights were men of some substance, having both lands and revenues as sources of income. Only one knight seems to have had allodial lands, most holding theirs dependently as fiefs from their lords, but not enough sources survive to permit a conclusive judgment on this matter, nor even on the size of their possessions.[73] To judge by their names a few knights such as Pagan of le Palais near Parthenay lived in rural hamlets, but most, including those about whom most is known, lived in the castles of the region. Guy of Ternant came from that castle and others like Rainier Faber, Urias, Geoffrey Boliau, and William Sanxon had houses in Parthenay castle.[74] But this does not eliminate the possibility of their having had country homes as well. Nor were they men to be trifled with or pushed around easily. Urias of Parthenay, a knight of Ralph Malclavel around 1100, defied monks, the Bishop of Poitiers, and excommunication, in a dispute over a tithe, not relenting until bribed with the large sum of 340 shillings.[75] Another knight named Bouchard, a vassal of the lord of Parthenay, was chosen by the latter to take over the important fief of Geoffrey Gilbert when Geoffrey died without heirs, around 1150.[76]

Similar as they were in so many respects to nobles of the Gâtine, were the knights of the region actually members of the nobility?

[72] Cartulaires de l'Absie, p. 20.
[73] Chartes de St. Maixent, I, 213. In this respect the knights of the Gâtine appear to have differed from their counterparts in Forez as studied by M. Perroy and in the Maconnais as studied by M. Duby. G. Duby, " Une enquête à poursuivre: la noblesse dans la France médiévale," Revue Historique, 1961, pp. 1–22.
[74] Cartulaire de Talmond, pp. 173–75. Chartes de St. Maixent, I, 213. Archives de Maine-et-Loire, Série 101H225 bis, No. 192.
[75] Cartulaire de Talmond, pp. 173–75.
[76] Ibid., pp. 294–95.

Given the lacunae of the documents which cast a shadow of uncertainty on any assertion, the most satisfactory answer to this question is that the knights were definitely not nobles, but seem to have been men in the process of pushing their way into its ranks. The evidence of titles is decisive on the existence of a distinction, as is the condition of close dependence of most knights on nobles.[77] Even more conclusive is the peasant origin of at least some knights, such as Martin of Foussais, who was a *miles*, but also a *homo consuetudinarius*, or a man subject to customs as only peasants were.[78] Two other men who lived in the later part of the eleventh century and who bore the title of knight, originally were *prévôts*, or peasant officials of considerable importance, who somehow succeeded in exchanging the one status for the other; and a fourth was the son of a parish priest.[79] In all probability many knights came from such a background, thus making low birth a factor which separated them from the nobility.[80] Despite this they were far above the peasantry, and, as has been demonstrated, were often barely distinguished from the nobility in power and manner of life.[81] Their superiority may have been sometimes temporary and precarious, as in the case of Odo whose weapons were confiscated for failure to fight in a duel, but there are strong suggestions that knighthood was becoming a hereditary condition and not something dependent exclusively on personal skill. At least one and probably two sons of Rainier Faber, a knight of

[77] Dependence on a lord is, in itself, of course no criterion for exclusion from the nobility since all noblemen themselves were vassals of the lord of Parthenay. Never in his charters, however, did he refer to a nobleman as his vassal, or his man, as the nobleman did to his knight. Such language implies that the latter relationship was closer and more restrictive than the former.

[78] Bibliothèque de la ville de Tours, *Abbaye de Bourgueil: Recueil de titres relatifs à l'abbaye de Bourgueil ou essai de reconstitution d'un ancien cartulaire* (Collection of André Salmon, 2 volumes, MSS 1338, 1339), I, 262.

[79] *Cartulaire de Talmond*, pp. 164, 168, 175. *Cartulaire de Cormery*, p. 91. Bibliothèque Nationale, Gaignières, F. L. 17127, p. 379. *Cartulaires du Bas-Poitou*, p. 93. *Chartes de St. Maixent*, I, 244, 382.

[80] It may well be, as M. Jean Richard has found in Burgundy, that knights of a castle were of peasant origin whereas those from country hamlets or villages, as indicated by their names, came from minor noble stock. Jean Richard, " Châteaux, châtelains, et vassaux en Bourgogne aux XIᵉ et XIIᵉ siècles," *Cahiers de civilisation médiévale* (1960), p. 441.

[81] Monastic scribes of this period occasionally took care to divide witnesses to charters into "knights and all others," a sure sign that men were impressed by the differences between the two groups. For example a charter of the end of the eleventh century ends in the following way; ". . . videntibus istis; Fulcherio

the Roux of Parthenay, were knights, and *miles* is attached to a family named Sanxon from 1070 through the twelfth century.[82]

In 1197 the head of an old noble house of the northern Gâtine called himself, ". . . P. Maingoti, miles, dominus de Chocaroia . . .," or Peter Maingot, knight, and lord of la Chausserais, and in so doing pointed to a breakdown of the barriers between knights and nobles.[83] The increasing use of *miles* by nobility after that time shows that the ability to fight as an armed knight on horseback was becoming an essential feature of nobility, a feature on which much greater emphasis was placed than in the eleventh century.[84] On one earlier occasion a knight did succeed in a very striking fashion to an important noble estate in the northeastern Gâtine. In 1150 Geoffrey Gilbert of Lamairé died, apparently without direct descendants, and his fief escheated to the lord of Parthenay. William of Parthenay, despite the bitter protests of collateral relatives, gave it to one of his knights, ". . . a certain knight by the name of Bouchard . . .," as a monk of Talmond described him.[85] Taking over command of the fief Bouchard started impressively by presiding over his seigneurial court, but it is impossible to ascertain whether he kept the estate and passed it on to his heirs, or, in other words, whether he perpetuated his newly acquired status. A cursory glance through printed sources reveals that the assimilation of knights into the nobility was sufficiently advanced by 1269 that the lord of Parthenay used the title for the first time.[86] But only a careful check of thirteenth-century records, if indeed

monacho, Giraldo Rufo, item Giraldo juveni, Rainaldo Crasso; de militibus vero: Simone de Sunlis, Rainaldo Bene se vestit, Fulcone capellano et aliis pluribus. . . ." *Cartulaire de Talmond*, p. 173.

[82] *Ibid.* How men became knights is never portrayed in contemporary documents, thus leaving obscure the matter as to whether the status of knighthood was open to anyone properly armed and trained, or was a privilege available only to sons of knights.

[83] *Chartes de St. Maixent*, I, 383. A similar combination of *miles* and *dominus* occurred around the same time in a charter involving Boers, lord of Champdeniers. *Chartes de Nouaille*, p. 343.

[84] In witnessing a charter of 1192 Simon Maingot, a brother or relative of Peter Maingot, lord of la Chausserais, and William Sanxon, a descendant of an eleventh-century family of *prévôts* of the lord of Parthenay, were classified side by side as knights. *Chartes de St. Maixent*, I, 382.

[85] ". . . Tunc miles quidam, Bucardus nomine, filius Petri Droconis, honorem et possessionem memorati Gausfridi Gilberti dono et concessione Willelmi Archiepiscopi injuste rapuit et obtinuit. . . ." *Cartulaire de Talmond*, pp. 294–95.

[86] J. Besly, *Histoire*, p. 400.

they are extensive enough, could show whether in actual fact the descendants of twelfth-century knights headed noble dynasties.

The preceding discussion will have suggested that birth was a more important criterion for nobility than the ability to fight. That the nobility was already, when first encountered, an hereditary class into which one was born, is well established. The continuous histories of the earliest families known, those of Verruyes, Malclavel, la Chapelle-Thireuil, and especially Parthenay, put it beyond doubt. Moreover, it was a class fully conscious of its separation from the rest of society and its members quite naturally married exclusively among themselves. An alliance with someone of inferior station would have been considered degrading and moreover might conceivably have allowed a new family to move up beyond its proper place. With an extremely limited number of families furnishing eligible marriage partners—some people, of course, married into houses outside the region—the result was a high degree of interrelationship between the noble families of the Gâtine. As an illustration one may consider the five noble lines prominent in the parishes of Lamairé, la Peyratte, and Parthenay, which over a fifty year period from 1100–50 had all become related by marriage. The two leading families, the Gilbert's and the Chabot's, were united when William Chabot married Petronilla Gilbert sometime just before 1100. At the same time the Gilbert's were somehow related to Maingaud of Parthenay and his wife, who in turn were connected with the family of Audeard Roux of Parthenay. Finally a marriage around 1150 between Margaret, a niece of Ralph Malclavel, and Simon Roux linked those two families.[87] Even though family ties are more difficult to reconstruct in other parishes because of scantier documentation, they were no doubt just as complex as in Lamairé and la Peyratte, and went far to create a community of interests between most of the nobility of the region.

A hereditary class it certainly was, but probably not a closed, exclusive one into which entry was barred except by birth. Certain families such as the lords of Allonne did not become prominent until the early twelfth century, a prominence which may result from their having been newly founded at that time. More likely, however, this is simply the consequence of a lack of records for

[87] *Cartulaire de Talmond*, pp. 164–67, 281, 282. *Cartulaires de l'Absie*, p. 62.

the western Gâtine for the period prior to the second quarter of the twelfth century. On the other hand the progressive merging of nobles and knights into a single class in the later twelfth and thirteenth centuries certainly implies that the latter came to be regarded as nobles, but proof of this awaits further study.

Thus birth, greater wealth and power, and a highly distinctive way of life singled out the nobles from the rest of the society of the Gâtine. How these men rose to that position of eminence, or what were the origins of the nobility, is a problem of almost impenetrable obscurity. The clear separation between knights and nobles, at least until 1175, proves that the latter were not men whose ability to arm themselves and fight enabled them to push to the top of society in the later tenth and eleventh centuries when public government disintegrated.[88] But the lack of records for the period prior to 1000 makes it impossible to either prove or disprove the more recent theory that the nobility of the eleventh and twelfth centuries were the descendants of old, long-recognized families dating well back into Carolingian times in the ninth century.[89] The continuous occupation of the Gâtine during the ninth and tenth centuries makes this possible, but the partial depopulation of the region as a result of invasions makes it unlikely that all the noble lines of the later period reach back through this earlier one. As previously noted, the family of Parthenay was probably new to the region around the year 1000. It is well known that at this time the counts of Anjou and Poitou and the viscounts of Thouars were endowing their followers with lands and castles in Bas-Poitou, including the Gâtine, for the purpose of colonization and defense. Thus it seems at least likely that a significant number of noble families began as the beneficiaries of this policy.

The wealth of many noble families in other parts of France was seriously threatened in the eleventh century by division and alienation of their lands, and there are indications that such a development also took place in the Gâtine.[90] Most notable of these was the tendency of individual noble families to form closely

---

[88] The theory of Marc Bloch, *La société féodale*, II, 1–15.

[89] The theory of Karl F. Werner. See above, p. 45, footnote 8.

[90] On this phenomenon in the Maconnais see Duby, *La société*, pp. 47–63; and in the county of Namur see Léopold Genicot, *L'économie rurale Namuroise au bas moyen âge*, Vol. 1, *La seigneurie foncière* (Recueil de travaux d'histoire et de philologie de l'Université de Louvain, 3rd Series, 17th fascicule), Chapter 2.

knit units which in size came to include collateral relatives as
well as the parents and children and which carefully scrutinized
and controlled the activities of each one of its members. In this
way they hoped to preserve their territorial holdings, the economic
basis for their elevated rank in society. One problem was created
by the propensity of many families to reproduce prolifically, often
leaving several sons who needed land to support their military
ventures and daughters for whom marriage dowries had to be
provided.[91] The matter of dowries could be alleviated somewhat
if some of the female heirs could be persuaded to dedicate themselves to the religious life in a convent, an action which was as
pious as it was practical. The famous monastery of Fontevrault
counted many noblewomen from the Gâtine, such as the daughter
of Simon II of Parthenay, among the nuns in its order in the
twelfth century.[92] Many a nobleman must also have followed
the example of the Lord of Billy in 1154 who gave his son a
career in a monastery and thereby eased his own burden of providing for many male heirs.[93]

It was to meet this as well as other problems that the lords of
Parthenay adopted the system of inheritance called the *droit de
viage et retour* at the middle of the eleventh century.[94] By allowing
each brother to enjoy the proceeds of a small part of the family
property, but preventing him from turning it over to his heirs,
the *droit de viage* reinforced the principle of nondivision even
more strictly than primogeniture and averted the dissolution of
that property. As a result the younger members of a family
tended to remain by their eldest brother and assist in the administration of the lands which they could one day expect to rule
themselves. Thus at any given time a noble household might
include the head with his wife and children, some of whom had
children of their own, and his brothers and their families;
altogether an entire community.[95] Although unequivocal proof of

[91] Families of five, six, and seven children were quite common in the Gâtine in
this period. Peter Gerard, lord of Chiché, had four sons and three daughters, Garins
of Bonnay had seven boys, and William I of Parthenay had five sons and one
daughter. Archives de Maine-et-Loire, Série 101H225, No. 789. *Cartulaires de
l'Absie, pp.* 22, 26. *Chartes de St. Maixent,* I, 247. *Cartulaire de Saintes,* II, 143–44.
[92] Archives de Maine-et-Loire, Série 187H1, No. 1.
[93] *Ibid.,* Série 101H225 bis, No. 396.
[94] See above, p. 51.
[95] Thus Ebbo and Gelduin of Parthenay and their wives, children, nephews, and
posterity witnessed the foundation charter of Parthenay-le-Vieux in 1092. ". . . Hanc

it is lacking, the *droit de viage* was almost certainly adhered to by some of the lesser nobility after the example of the house of Parthenay.[96]

Another serious threat to the integrity of noble patrimonies arose from the pressing and quite unavoidable obligation of the nobleman to donate something to the church on any number of occasions, more especially when a church or a burg was founded, or when he was about to die. In his zeal to be generous to the church a noble could easily strip his estates of so much land and so many revenues that his descendants would be unable to continue living in the style demanded by their class. In the eleventh century the generosity of some seigneurs to the church was most impressive, as for example Simon of Verruyes who around 1040 gave St. Maixent two churches, one burg, nine manses of land, and some incidental revenues, or Ralph the Flame who donated four churches, four manses, a burg, and some other revenues to St. Cyprien around 1040.[97] The twelfth century brought an abrupt end to lavish donations of that kind which were probably more than any single estate could afford. Almost never did anyone give as much as a single manse of land. Instead people limited their gifts to *borderia*'s or much more often, just revenues of insignificant amounts. Quite typical of the relative niggardliness of the twelfth-century nobility was the donation made by William II, lord of Parthenay himself, to help in the founding of the monastery of l'Absie. No lands at all were included in the grant which was nothing more than twenty shillings yearly, plus a tithe and freedom from road and sales taxes for all monks and lay brothers of the monastery.[98] This is scarcely the generosity one would expect of a powerful baron like the lord of the Gâtine,

donationem, nos Gelduinus et Ebo, et uxores nostrae, et filii nostri, et nepotes nostri, Guillelmus et Simon, et posteris nostris, ut scripta est, tenendam relinquimus. . . ." Besly, *Histoire*, p. 396.

[96] For example, sometime around 1070, after Aimeri Pulzin had given the church of St. Laurs to the abbey of Bourgueil, first his brother, then his wife and three sons gave their consent to his act. The best explanation for the precedence of the brother over the wife and sons is that the former stood ahead of the latter in the line of succession, which was of course the main characteristic of the *droit de viage*. *Mémoires de la société de statistique des Deux-Sèvres* (2nd series, XIV, 1875), 283–84. *Cartulaires de l'Absie*, p. 18. P. Portejoie, *Le régime des fiefs*, p. 124.

[97] *Chartes de St. Maixent*, I, 120–21. *Cartulaire de St. Cyprien*, p. 106.

[98] *Cartulaires de l'Absie*, pp. 2, 81.

but one can easily infer that he, like the rest of the nobility, had been forced to economize.

From the later eleventh century on, every alienation of land or revenues, no matter how insignificant it was, required the approval of all the members of the immediate family and often those of collateral branches. For instance, when Maingaud of Parthenay and his wife donated the tithe of all their vineyards in Lamairé to the abbey of Talmond around 1115, no less than three generations gave their consent to it; William Gilbert, archdeacon of Poitiers, his mother Elizabeth, his brother Geoffrey Gilbert, and sister Petronilla and the latter's husband, William Chabot, and their two sons Brient and Chabot.[99] Moreover any grant made without the consent of those relatives was invalid as the church learned to its sorrow time after time when a man's descendants contested what he had done. Such disputes arose particularly often when a man who was dying tried to amend for his past life by being over-generous to the church, something which clergymen naturally made no effort to discourage. It was under those circumstances that Maingaud of Parthenay bestowed some land on the abbot of Talmond, but on the very day he died one of his relatives claimed it had been unjustly given and the case was not settled until, after much litigation and arguing, the abbot returned one-third of the land and paid Ebbo of Parthenay six pounds, to boot, for protection.[100] In the long run the alarming frequency of disputes over alienated property both dampened the enthusiasm of the donor and made the church profoundly skeptical of accepting anything without the express consent of all relatives. In some instances churchmen went to extreme lengths to insure that no contestations could possibly materialize. The case of Urias of Parthenay admittedly involved a man of knightly and not noble status, but the problem of preserving family lands intact was common to members of all classes in this period. In 1100 when Urias, a vassal of Ralph Malclavel, finally came to terms with the abbot of Talmond after a disagreement over a tithe, the latter first secured the promise of Ralph and Urias to abide by the settlement through the payments of 340 *solidi* and a silver cup. Urias' brother Frotier also gave his consent, but since Urias' wife was then in childbirth, three monks had to be sent to her

[99] *Cartulaire de Talmond*, pp. 281, 282.
[100] *Ibid.*, p. 173.

bedside for her approval. The abbot next sought the assent of
their children, but not until after the passage of quite some time
and two separate trips to Parthenay did he find all three of them.[101]
No doubt the church found it intensely irritating to have its hands
bound so often by the control which the familial group exercised
over the actions of its head and members, but at the same time it
is equally certain that that restraint prevented the splintering of
many a noble inheritance and saved not a few from eventual
dissolution.

What has been written until now applies to the nobility in
general with the reservation that substantial variations in wealth
differentiated some families from others and kept the class from
being completely uniform.[102] Nonetheless, all were vassals of the
lord of Parthenay, none having his own castle, and all exercised
approximately the same kind of power over their peasants. Foremost among the nobility of the Gâtine and, in fact in a class by
himself, was the lord of Parthenay. To him belonged most of the
region either in *domaine* or in fief. Every nobleman who lived
in the shadow of one of his castles of Parthenay, Secondigny,
Champdeniers, and the two lesser ones, owed him homage and
held a fief from him. As commander of those castles, he alone
could police the main roads of the Gâtine, guarantee safe conduct
for travelers, and punish violators of the public peace. In other
words the most vital of the sovereign powers which had formerly
been held by the count as the public representative of the Carolingian state, were now the personal property of the lord of
Parthenay. In recognition of this lofty position the lord of
Parthenay alone among the nobility took the title *dominus*, or
lord, or seigneur.[103]

---

[101] *Ibid.*, pp. 173–75.

[102] Consider for instance the contrast between the Malclavel's and the lords of
Vernoux as discussed above, p. 85.

[103] Only at the end of the twelfth century did two other nobles, the lords of la
Chausserais and of Champdeniers, use this title. See above, page 95, footnote 83.

CHAPTER IV

PEASANTS AND THE *SEIGNEURIE*

The most numerous element in the medieval society of the Gâtine was that of the peasants. Not necessarily the best-known element, however, since very often they figure merely as names and nothing more in witness lists at the end of contemporary charters. This happened because the wealthier nobility had more occasion to donate something to churches and thus issue charters than did peasants. Nonetheless, enough indirect information is available to demonstrate that whereas it counted for little politically the peasantry did provide the economic basis for life in the region.

The peasantry stood out from the rest of medieval society in that its members made their living by cultivating the soil. In attempts to capture the essential traits of this class contemporaries employed several terms of description, but most of them emphasized its argicultural character. In many instances the peasant was called a *rupturarius*, a *roturier* in French, or one who cultivates the land. Several other terms referred more specifically to the rural character of the peasantry; a *rusticus* was a man who lived in the country away from dense conglomerations of people. In contrast to those who settled in towns or burgs, he often was known as a *villanus*, or an inhabitant of a *villa*, one of the tiny villages or hamlets of the Gâtine. Another word of very great antiquity and in common usage was *colonus* or, generally speaking, any peasant. Finally, there were several other nouns such as *parrochianus*, parishioner, and *habitator*, inhabitant, which had a more general descriptive value and were void of any exact signification.[1]

---

[1] *Cartulaires de l'Absie*, pp. 7, 38, 48, 64, 65, 67, 88, 95, 101, 120, 127. *Cartulaire de St. Cyprien*, pp. 114, 309. Bibliothèque Nationale, Gaignières, F. L. 17127, pp. 127–28. Bibliothèque de Tours, Collection Salmon, MS 1338, p. 301. Archives de Maine-et-Loire, Série 101H225, No. 789.

Land, livestock, and sometimes vineyards were the economic resources of peasants of the region. Since substantial variations in wealth existed among different families of this class it is difficult to speak of the average peasant holding, but easily the most common agricultural unit of this period was the *borderia*, a unit probably ranging in size from two to fifteen *hectares*, or five to thirty-seven acres.[2] Although the *borderia*, a self-contained farm with fields, woods, and a meadow, clearly sufficed to maintain a single family, the frequency of references to smaller fields, such as the *sextaria* of about two and one-half acres, fosters the notion that peasants could live on less.[3] Whatever the minimum amount necessary to support a peasant family may have been, and whatever the actual average, it is perfectly clear that some had much more and lived in relative opulence.

In evaluating the economic condition of the medieval peasant the size of his land is the foremost consideration, but of vital importance was the status of that land, whether it was an allod, that is a freehold, or a tenure. Unlike the nobility, few peasants appear to have had allods, most renting their lands from a landlord.[4] The colonization of the region actually contributed to the creation of new ones for when seigneurs entered into contracts of complant with peasants for the culture of grapevines, they surrendered half the vines to the latter at the time when grapes were produced.[5] Regardless of size, the peasant tenure most commonly was called a *roture*, *ruptura*, from the fact that it was worked by a *rupturarius* or one who breaks the soil, but peasant fiefs were not rare.[6] In any event, revenues in money and kind constituted the principal part of the rent for both. The *terrage*, from the latin *terra* or land, was a widespread land tax. Originally a percentage of the yield of the land, varying in other parts of France from one-fourth to one-twelfth, the *terrage* seems to have become a fixed tax by the end of the twelfth century, paid both

[2] See above p. 36.

[3] On the size of the *sextaria*, Merle, *La métairie*, p. 42.

[4] Examples of peasant allods, *Cartulaire de Talmond*, p. 169. *Cartulaires de l'Absie*, p. 14.

[5] Duby, *Économie rurale*, II, 378–79. See below, p. 104.

[6] ". . . Dederunt rupturam unam masuram terrae . . ." *ibid.*, p. 95. ". . . terram illam quam ipsi habebant feodaliter ab eodem Aimerico hoc tamen tenore quod ipsa ecclesia inde illis eorumque successoribus terragium solummodo redderet. . . ." Bibliothèque Nationale, Gaignières, F. L. 5480, p. 136.

in money and kind.[7] In at least one case lord and peasant halved the fruits of the soil whatever they might be. Such tenures, known as *métairies*, from the latin *medietas* signifying one-half the produce, were rare in eleventh and twelfth centuries, but by the sixteenth century they had come to far outnumber all other types of agricultural exploitation.[8]

The agreement to settle for one-half the produce was particularly widespread insofar as the cultivation of grapes for wine was concerned. The stipulation of several seigneurs to the effect that the vineyards which they were giving to churches would continue to pay tithe even if some other crop should be substituted for the grapes, leaves no doubt that viticulture was an even more hazardous business than agriculture, primarily no doubt because of the very damp climate and soil.[9] In any event the vines could not begin to produce until several years after planting and for this reason vineyards were commonly leased to peasants under a contract of complant—*complantum*—which meant that the seigneur would receive one-half the grapes whenever there was a harvest.[10]

Some peasants owed a land tax called the *cens* which, like the *terrage*, was attached to recently cleared fields, but was fixed in amount from the first and payable both in money and kind.[11]

[7] ". . . Goscelinus abbas et totus conventus donavimus et concedimus Bernardo Garnes et heredibus ejus, in hereditatem perpetuam, arbergamentum Berauderiae et terram unam scilicet borderiatam. De his reddunt decimam et terragium de XX solidis per annum et decimam omnium bestiarum et adjutorium boum et quadrigariarum suarum quod biannum vocatur, sicuti alii homines nostri nobis facient. . . ." *Cartulaires de l'Absie*, p. 79.

[8] ". . . Ego Ermengodus . . . dedi . . . meteriam meam de Mazeriis, quam agricolabat Martinus mercenarius meus. . . ." *Chartes de St. Maixent*, I, 231. L. Merle, *La métairie et l'évolution agraire de la Gâtine Poitevine* (Paris, 1958). In this book Dr. Merle has traced the agricultural history of the Gâtine and the development of the *métairie* from the sixteenth through the eighteenth centuries.

[9] ". . . concesserunt etiam ut in utraque parrochia, quecumque terra eorum semel plantata esset in vineas, si postea extirparentur vinee non minus ob hoc terra illa ulterius decimam de annona et de aliis rebus monachis redderet . . .," *Cartulaire de Talmond*, p. 167.

[10] ". . . postmodum concesserunt Gaufridus Gilberti . . . partem quam in eadem vinea habebant, id est complantum . . .," *ibid.*, p. 168.

[11] Examples of *cens* paid in kind, *Cartulaire de Talmond*, p. 171; *Cartulaires de l'Absie*, pp. 25, 95; and in money, *ibid.*, pp. 24, 66, 102, 110, 111, etc. In one case a single tenure owed both *terrage* and *cens*. *Ibid.*, p. 1. Duby, *L'économie rurale*, II, 440–41.

In the northeastern Gâtine where wheat could be cultivated, it was labeled *frumentage* from the name for that grain.[12]

Among the heaviest of the taxes affecting the peasantry was the tithe, or tenth part, which every peasant paid on all his crops and livestock. Normally assumed to belong to the local parish priest and church, the tithe in practice invariably went to the noblemen and sometimes even peasants in the parish. Despite the concerted, and occasionally successful, efforts of the churches and monasteries of the region to obtain the rich returns of this offering, it continued for the most part to be held by laymen.[13]

Weighing further on all peasants, although in this instance on them as individuals instead of on their land, was the obligation to pay the parish priest for each of the religious services which he rendered to them. Among these were the offering for Sunday Mass, baptism, confession, marriage, and burial in the church cemetery, all of which were sometimes grouped under the collective term *parrochiam*.[14]

Nearly every seigneur reserved the best land, the largest woods, and the streams on his property for his own uses and recreation, but most were willing to allow their tenants temporary usage of them in return for various revenues which French historians call the *droits d'usage*, or rights of usage. Even though most peasant exploitations had at least a small bit of woods, this was apparently not sufficient for the needs of many tenants who used part of their seigneur's extensive reserves for pasturing their pigs.[15] Peasants were also permitted to take wood from those forests for building as well as heating purposes, but they paid a healthy

---

[12] ". . . dono in elemosinam modium frumenti ad Auream Vallem de frumentagio meo . . ." *ibid.*, p. 113.

[13] The cartularies of l'Absie, Talmond, and St. Maixent are filled with acts recording the donation of the tithe of nearby parishes by the men who had hitherto had possession of it. It was one of the most highly valued of all seigneurial revenues and claims to it precipitated far more disputes between churchmen and lay society than anything else, not to mention several heated battles between monasteries of the region. For an example of the first kind see above, p. 100, and for the second, *Cartulaire de Talmond*, pp. 287–89.

[14] Bibliothèque de Tours, Collection Salmon, MS 1338, p. 301. Around 1100 the church of Lamairé was given to the abbey of Talmond, ". . . cum omnibus que ad eam pertinebant, scilicet offerendam, sepulturam, baptisterium, confessiones, et . . .," *Cartulaire de Talmond*, p. 164.

[15] *Pastio, pasquerium*, and *pasturalia* were the different terms used to designate the tax paid for pasturage of animals. *Cartulaires de l'Absie*, p. 91. *Cartulaire de Cormery*, pp. 90–93.

revenue for the privilege. When Thibaud of Bressuire granted certain forest rights at a place near Chiché in the northern Gâtine to the monks of St. Jouin, around 1090, he laid down the conditions that they could take dry or fallen wood from the grove of Blandochet at any time of the year, and that in the time of the acorns, "in tempore glandis," they might pasture one hundred of their own pigs.[16] Permission to use the seignurial forest for building materials was always sought after by settlers who needed wood for their houses, their church, and a mill.[17] Upon receipt of a revenue known variously as *piscatio, piscaria,* and *piscatura,* some seigneurs let people fish on their ponds and rivers, but one wonders if this were not an exclusive right of the monastic orders of the Gâtine and quite out of reach of most ordinary peasants.[18] The seigneur also charged for other facilities which he provided for peasant use, namely his mills, oven, and wine press.[19]

The prevalence of tenures and the rarity of allods thus reveals that the peasants of the Gâtine were economically dependent on landlords who were usually nobility. Or in other words, that the *seigneurie,* or seigneurial system, was firmly established in the region. However, the *seigneurie foncière,* as French and Belgian historians call it, of this period cannot be equated with the onerous *domaine* system, or *régime domaniale,* of Carolingian times, but was a creation of the colonization of the eleventh and twelfth centuries. Most of the settlements of the tenth and early eleventh centuries did in fact receive the name *villa,* the term commonly used to describe the large estate of the Carolingian era. Likewise, the characteristic name for the peasant holding in the Carolingian estate, manse, was attached to most tenures of the eleventh century. On the other hand, *villa,* already in the tenth century, appears often to have meant simply village, or any cluster of houses, and not necessarily the estate of a single owner.[20] Added

[16] *Chartularium Sancti Jovini,* p. 24.

[17] ". . . dedit etiam Simon Sancto Paulo licentiam de silvis suis faciendi omne quodcumque necessarium ad domos faciendos, ad molendinum, ad calefaciendum furnum, ad clausuram burgi et agrorum, pastionem ad porcos dominicos . . .," *Cartulaire de Cormery,* pp. 90–93.

[18] ". . . dedit quoque licentiam piscandi in flumine Trato apud Partheniacum, et in stagno apud Secundiniacum unum piscatorem ad usum monachorum. . . ." *Ibid.*

[19] The fee for milling grains was named *mosdura,* whereas it was *pressoragium* for the use of the wine press. *Cartulaire de Talmond,* p. 346. *Cartulaires de l'Absie,* p. 5.

[20] ". . . hoc est de terra et villa et ecclesia de Campellis. . . ." *Chartes de St.*

to this, contemporaries gradually discarded both of these terms during this period, with *villa* disappearing after 1050 and manse becoming uncommon after 1100. This clearly implies a breakdown of the *villa* and to a lesser degree the manse. Finally the heavy obligation of Carolingian peasants to work several days a week farming their lord's *domaine* was either restricted or nonexistent in the eleventh and twelfth centuries. The monks of l'Absie required an unspecified amount of *corvées* of their tenants in the later twelfth century, but no other seigneur in the region ever mentioned it.[21] Consequently if, as seems likely, some of the peasant tenures of this period did derive from the Carolingian *villa*, their tenants had succeeded in largely eliminating the *corvée*.

By far the greatest number of tenures resulted from the clearing and cultivation of wooded or waste land. The name used to describe them, *borderia*, and the taxes levied on them, *terrage* and *cens*, both had wide circulation in other parts of medieval France at this time to designate new farms.[22] Thus with a minimal number of taxes to pay plus relative freedom from *corvées*, and an hereditary claim to their land, peasants on these new farms were not excessively burdened by dependence on a *seigneur foncier*, for their relationship to him was fundamentally one of tenant to landlord, not one of personal subjection.

But this was not the end of the peasant's dependence on a superior. In the eleventh century the establishment of the barony of Parthenay, largely independent of the public authority of the count of Poitou, profoundly affected the agricultural classes. For the lords of Parthenay, solidly entrenched behind the walls of their several castles, gradually usurped the governmental powers of the count and began to exercise them over the population in the vicinity of their fortifications. The landed aristocracy they persuaded to become their feudal vassals, and at the same time they exerted coercion of a far different nature over the peasantry. Based on their ability to command and punish as if they were

Maixent, I, 157. Here *villa* seems to refer just to the houses as distinct from the surrounding fields. ". . . cedimus . . . alodum nostrum, qui est in pago pictavensi, in vicaria Toarcinse, in ville que dicitur Valerius. . . ." An allod in this *villa* points to more than one owner of land there. *Ibid.*, p. 89. See also, Henri Dubled, "Quelques observations sur le sens du mot *villa*," *Le Moyen Age* (1953), pp. 1–11.

[21] See above, p. 104, footnote 7.

[22] Latouche, *The Birth of Western Economy*, pp. 292–93. Duby, *L'économie rurale*, II, 440–41.

public officials, and manifested in the submission of the peasant to numerous exactions and restrictions, this power amounted to a new form of *seigneurie* superimposed over that of the *seigneurie foncière*. In attempting to point out its essential characteristics, various modern historians have given it different names such as *seigneurie banale, seigneurie hautaine,* and *seigneurie rurale.*[23] The one emphasizes the lord's *bannum,* or power of command, the second, his possession of high justice, and the last the fact that he exercised his authority over an entire rural area, not just within the confines of a single estate. The basic difference between the two forms of *seigneurie* was that the latter affected the inhabitants of all peasant lands within the castellany, or territory around the castle, and involved much more than the economic dependence of the *seigneurie foncière.* The obligations imposed by the seigneur *banal* or territorial lord were known as customs, *consuetudines,* from the fact that they came in time to be justified by custom or tradition. Although they sometimes distinguished between revenues owed to a landlord and customs owed to a territorial lord, the men of the time usually employed the term *dominium,* meaning the power exercised by the lord, *dominus,* and rendered by lordship in English and by *seigneurie* in French, to describe both kinds of *seigneurie* combined.[24]

The process by which lords levied customs and established the territorial *seigneurie* cannot be followed in detail, but it clearly began at the start of the century, with the first reference to *consuetudines* dating from 1003.[25] Rarely do the sources reveal how seigneurs collected customs, most often simply registering a *fait accompli.* However, since they lacked any legitimate justification for their action, some employed force to extract these taxes from peasants who consequently detested them as a sign of degradation

[23] Duby, *La société,* pp. 205 f. Robert Boutruche, *Seigneurie et féodalité,* Vol. 1, *Le premier âge des liens d'homme à homme.* Aubier, Collection historiques (Paris, 1959), pp. 114 f.

[24] ". . . similiter quoque facerent monachi ita ut deinceps omnes terrae redditus et omnes consuetudines. . . ." Bibliothèque de Tours, Collection Salmon, MS 1339, No. 30. Here revenues and customs are differentiated. ". . . et concedo ut quicquid iuris et dominii . . . in illo quarterone terre habui. . . ." Archives de Maine-et-Loire, Série 187H1, No. 1.

[25] On the imposition of customs and the *seigneurie banale* in France at large, see J.-F. Lemarignier, " La dislocation du *Pagus* et le problème des *Consuetudines* (X°-XI° siècles)," *Mélanges d'histoire dédiés à la mémoire de Louis Halphen* (Paris, 1951), pp. 401–11; and R. Boutruche, *Seigneurie et féodalité,* pp. 114–26.

and humiliation. Around 1100 a certain Savary was prevailed upon to renounce the evil custom " *consuetudinem malam*," which he had unjustly demanded in Largeasse, a custom, moreover, which had never before been required of the local inhabitants.[26] In this instance pressure applied by the abbot of Bourgueil deterred a seigneur from extorting a custom from some peasants of the monks, but one may be sure that much of the time the latter had no protector and were unsuccessful in resisting.

After 1100 the term " custom " appears in great profusion in the charters showing that the installation of the territorial *seigneurie* was far advanced if not complete, and that the public authority of the count of Poitou had been excluded from all but a tiny corner of the southwestern Gâtine which was his own *domaine*. In one sense Count William the Great (993–1030) himself contributed to his loss of power, for in granting to monasteries of Poitou several large estates in the southwestern Gâtine together with full immunity from comital government, he was in effect creating new ecclesiastical seigneuries which were totally removed from his control.[27] Furthermore, the fragmentation of public authority did not end with the usurpations of the lords of Parthenay, but spread rapidly through the feudal hierarchy until many lesser landlords had extracted customs from their peasant tenants. When such seigneurs donated land to the monasteries of the region they often stipulated, doubtless at the insistence of the monks, that henceforth it would be free of some or all of the customs its tenant owed.[28] Had this not been done, the

---

[26] ". . . Ego Savaricus non ignorans quam damnosum quam grave periculam necnon Deo et Sanctis ejus contrarium est elemosynam destruere vel consuetudines injustas priusque non habitas immictendo perturbare divina tandem inspiratione tactus, notum fieri volo omnibus hominibus tam futuris quam presentibus quod pro salute animae meae peccatorum meorum remissione commendalitiam et consuetudinem malam quam injuste expetebam et terra quae est apud Rajaciam . . .," Bibliothèque de Tours, Collection Salmon, MS 1338, p. 382.

[27] Around the end of the tenth century Count William created at least four *seigneuries immunistes* by giving the *villa*'s of St. Paul-en-Gâtine, Brettignolles, Scillé, and Germond in the western and southern Gâtine to the monks of Cluny and to the abbots of Bourgueil and of St. Cyprien. *Gallia Christiana*, 2, Instrumenta, Col. 331. Bibliothèque Nationale, Gaignières, F. L. 17127, pp. 127–28. Archives d'Indre-et-Loire, Série H24, MS No. 3. *Cartulaire de St. Cyprien*, p. 311.

[28] Two of many examples follow. ". . . Hugo de Grossa Cohanna et mater ejus Sofiza dederunt S. Cruci unam masuram terre, que vocatur Barrileria, ita libere et expedite ut nichil reddat tributarie consuetudinis, nisi tantummodo justissimam talleiam. . . ." *Cartulaire de Talmond*, p. 172. "Goscelinus Aminus et filii con-

peasant would have continued to pay the customs to his former lord and the monks would have lost an important part of the income from the land.

The nobility of the region collected a sizable number of customs on the basis of their usurped powers, not all by any means striking all peasants. The lords of Parthenay exacted the customs of *garda* and *custodia* as general protection taxes apparently over both lands and peasants, and over individuals on the road.[29] This custom was not confined to castellans, however, for two minor landlords in the northern Gâtine enjoyed proceeds from the *garda*.[30] *Commendize* was another similar and rather uncommon custom, and one held mostly by lesser lords. This resulted from the personal commendation of the peasant to a lord for the protection of himself and his land, and also reflects the insecurity of the period. Normally an amount of money, *commendize*, appears to have been levied according to the amount of land held by the peasant. When Papot Ermenard gave his land to the monastery of l'Absie around 1150 he stipulated that four *sextariata*'s of it should be left as marriage dowries for his two daughters who would pay four pennies of *commendize*, or one for each *sextariata* of land, to the monks each year. In the land of Brêchepote near Faye l'Abbesse, the lord, Andre Satanaz, assessed peasants twelve pennies of *commendize* for each ox team they possessed.[31]

In 1070 when he freed the men of the burg of St. Paul of Parthenay from the obligation of *bidamnum*, the Lord of Parthenay revealed that he, like castellans in other parts of France, had required peasants to perform certain work services, presumably the repair of his castles.[32] In all probability this was a usurpation

---

cesserunt totam terram de Berchepota de qua domus Absiae tunc erat investita, scilicet unam masuram et unam borderiam medietatis terrae d'Aujauri, liberas ab omni cosduma et servitio. . . ." *Cartulaires de l'Absie*, p. 93. Both these men were minor landlords; indeed, there is even some question as to whether the first was not simply a rich peasant!

[29] ". . . dono iterum illis et concedo cosdumas . . . gardam omnium euntium ad Absiam et redeuntium. . . ." *Ibid.*, pp. 81–82. ". . . et propter hoc dedit abbas domino Eboni VI libras denarorium Andegavorum, ut ipse eamdem terram et quidquid in eadem regione habebat sub custodia sua deffenderet." *Cartulaire de Talmond*, p. 173.

[30] *Cartulaires de l'Absie*, pp. 96, 112.

[31] *Ibid.*, pp. 46–47, 70.

[32] *Cartulaire de Cormery*, pp. 90–93. Duby, *L'économie rurale*, II, 453.

of a former prerogative of the count of Poitou.[33] Except for the abbot of l'Absie no other lord in the Gâtine held this power, and indeed, it cannot be known whether it touched all the peasants of the region.

It is beyond question that the most important of the governmental rights to be seized illegimately by the nobility of the Gâtine were those relating to the administration of justice. When the traditional courts of the count of Poitou ceased to function, the powers of public justice, the keeping of the peace, the apprehending, sentencing, and punishing of offenders became the function of a small body of nobility. But if the fact of private appropriation of the right of justice is beyond question, its distribution among the nobility is certainly not. Nor is it clear whether men regularly differentiated between low and high justice as they did in the thirteenth century, that is, between the right to try property disputes and minor misdemeanors and the right to judge cases involving capital punishment. If so, was high justice the exclusive prerogative of a few and not the many?

Some minor nobles like Geoffrey Gilbert of Lamairé plainly had at least the right to settle property disputes, but beyond this one must resort to hypothesis.[34] The custom designating the right of justice was *vicaria*, from the name of the former Carolingian judicial official, and it is likely, although not susceptible of proof, that the broader term *dominium*, or *seigneurie*, included justice among other powers. According to one contemporary scholar, *vicaria* comprehended both high and low justice, which could mean that several lower nobles of the region had the power of life and death over their peasants.[35] Relevant to this is a charter of the monastery of St. Maixent of around 1150 to the effect that Reginald of Allonne had been fined seven pounds by the Abbott for arbitrarily hanging a man.[36] Unfortunately, it is unclear

[33] Around the year 1000 it was normally expected of peasants that they perform " public works " for the count, one of which was the building of castles. ". . . insuper et coloni qui eas terras incolunt, ita sint ab omnibus publicis negotiis absoluti, ut nec ad castella facienda vel bidannum aliquod reddere, vel ipsi vel boves eorum cogantur. . . ." Bibliothèque Nationale, Gaignières, F. L. 17127, pp. 127–28.

[34] See above, p. 87.

[35] A. C. F. Koch, " L'origine de la haute et de la moyenne justice dans l'ouest et le nord de la France," *Tijdschrift vor Rechtsgeschiedenis* (1953), pp. 420–58. ". . . Gauterius Danjo concessit vicariam que sunt in feodo de Vernol. . . ." *Cartulaires de l'Absie*, pp. 6, 22.

[36] " Sciant presentes et futuri quod Reginaldus d'Alona est homo legius abbati

whether he incurred this punishment because he had no right to execute a peasant and was thus guilty of murder, or because he had executed him unjustly even though having the right of capital punishment.

At least one monastic *seigneurie* definitely did have full powers of justice, for when Count William of Poitou gave the monks of Bourgueil a priory at le Busseau in 1004, he specifically included the right of capital punishment in his grant.[37] Although there is no evidence of his exercising it, the lord of Parthenay, as the ruler of the region, obviously also had such authority, for he it was who in several instances permitted monks to judge the men of their newly settled burgs.[38] No restrictions were appended to these grants, but it still may be presumptuous to infer that the monks could judge all kinds of cases. The right of life and death may well have been the automatic monopoly of the greatest lay and ecclesiastical nobility. From the viewpoint of the medieval peasant all this was probably irrelevant, for in the final analysis he still had to submit to private instead of public justice.

A custom affecting many peasants through their lands and held by both castellans and nobility of lesser importance was the *taille*. Coming from a word meaning to take, *tollir*, the *taille* was a form of assistance taken by the seigneur both in money and kind. Sometimes it was an aid for unspecified purposes, simply *tallea*, but fairly often it served to assist the lord in the marriage of his daughter and as ransom money. Furthermore, the money peasants paid for the privilege of inheriting their tenures from their ancestors was also called a *taille, tallea de mortua manu*. Texts of the twelfth century indicate that, in a few instances at least, it was a fixed not an arbitrary amount.[39]

---

sancti Maxentii et placitum in voluntate ipsius abbatis, et ipse abbas P. Raimundus, pro eo quod in voluntate sua pendebat, accepit ab eo septem libras Andegavensis monete. . . ." *Chartes de St. Maixent*, I, 358-59.

[37] ". . . insuper non solum et in istis prenominatis . . . terris, sed etiam in omnibus prefati cenobi Burguliensi potestatibus vel terris . . . nullus ministerialis publicus nec prepositus nec . . . vicarius . . . neque pro sanguine, pro homicido, pro furtis, pro rapto, pro incendia . . . introeundi habeant potestam. . . ." Bibliothèque Nationale, Gaignières, F. L. 17127, pp. 127–28.

[38] *Ibid.*, p. 379. Besly, *Histoire*, p. 396. *Cartulaire de Cormery*, pp. 90–93.

[39] Duby, *L'économie rurale*, II, 454. ". . . Dono eisdem et concedo in elemosinam omnes terras et talleas earum. . . ." *Cartulaires des l'Absie*, p. 81. ". . . et dedi eis in eleemosynam rupturam unius masurae terrae quae erat de feodo Goffridi Vossart, concedentibus filiabus meis Peregrina et Angarde, taliter ut ipsa Peregrina et heredes

Should he ever go beyond the limits of his own farm, the peasant was subject to another set of customs quite apart from those levied on him through his land. Any individuals of non-noble status circulating on the roads of the region were required to pay the custom of *péage*, *pedagium*, from the latin *pes* and meaning one who goes afoot, to the lord of the castellany in which they happened to be. The task of policing the roads of the Gâtine, formerly a public function of the count, had been taken over by the several castellans of the region headed by the lord of Parthenay. Only they, in command of castles and military followers, had the means to guarantee safe passage over long distances.[40] Assuming that a peasant's purpose in journeying outside his own lands was to go to a market or a fair, he then had to pay to the seigneur who organized and regulated it, again normally a castellan, a sales tax called *venda*—from the latin *vendere*, to sell— on objects which he bought or sold.[41]

The imposition of the territorial *seigneurie* with its various customs could not avoid drastically altering the status of peasants of the Gâtine. In addition to their obligations to their landlord they now acquired new ones to the castellan and sometimes to still another lord who justified his authority by claiming to have replaced the count, and who backed it up ultimately with force. Peasants sometimes found that their landlords had now become as well their sovereign ruler who taxed them, issued orders to them, and punished them in matters which had little to do with the cultivation of the land. Dependence on several lords inevitably introduced an element of complexity and confusion into seigneurial relationships. Consider the example of Garnier Audebert, a peasant of the western Gâtine, who held a *borderia* of land from Giraud of la Loge Fougereuse, his landlord, but owed the custom of *commendize*, or commendation, to Fulk and Peter

---

sui, quamdiu vixerint, possideant quatuor sextariatas quas illis in maritagio dederam, pro quibus annuatim reddant fratribus de Massigne IV nummos de comendiza et XII de tallea, quotiens facta fuerit in ipsa masura a dominis feodi . . . Goffridus Vossart concessit hanc masuram terrae in eleemosinam fratribus Absiae . . . liberam a placito et ab omni cosduma, praeter terragium et talleam de mortua manu et de mariagio et de preisum. . . ." *Ibid.*, p. 47.

[40] The lords of Parthenay, Fôret-sur-Sèvre, Chiché, and viscount of Thouars were apparently the only nobility who collected the péage in or on the borders of the Gâtine. *Ibid.*, pp. 3, 67, 81, 134. *Chartularium Sancti Jovini*, p. 24. Besly, *Histoire*, p. 396.

[41] The same sources as for the preceding footnote.

Guesguent, of the ruling family of Vernoux.[42] Since nothing suggests that they held this custom as a fief from someone else, one must presume that Fulk and Peter, living in the vicinity of Garnier's lands, had forced him to accept their protection even though they were not his landlords. In another instance it is quite clear that the proximity of the castle of Bressuire to the *borderia* which Giraud Bornazels held from Ogier Eschot near l'Absie, enabled Peter Airaud, a relative of the Lord of that castle, to extort the same custom from Giraud.[43]

How seriously the territorial *seigneurie* weakened the economic resources of the peasants cannot be determined, but that through increased payments it resulted in a substantial deterioration is beyond question. Yet generally speaking it did not reduce them to serfdom. The language of the charters is of partial assistance in reaching this conclusion. Some of the tenth-century landlords of the Gâtine owned slaves, but never once during the eleventh and twelfth centuries is there a reference to a *servus* or serf.[44] But scholars have noticed a similar phenomenon, although of slightly later date, for other French provinces and have not interpreted this as necessarily meaning a disappearance of serfdom.[45] Rather the progressive merging of the classes of slaves and free peasants in the later Carolingian period, with a resulting amelioration in the condition of the one and a deterioration for the other, caused such a modification in the status of both that contemporaries devised new terms to describe them. The clear distinction of earlier times between free peasant and slave had vanished. As a result of the decline of public government and the spread of the territorial *seigneurie*, both became dependent on at least one and often several lords, making the similarities between their conditions more striking than the differences. Henceforth men used names which stressed the element of personal dependence, such as *homo proprius, homo tributerius*, and *manens*. Peasants were no longer simply freemen or serfs, they were more or less servile, the *homo proprius* more so than the *manens*.

[42] *Cartulaires de l'Absie*, pp. 95, 97.

[43] " Giraudus Bornazels dedit . . . unam borderiam terre, in hac terra habebat Petrus Airaudus de Berzorio commendizam et alias consuetudines. . . ." *Ibid.*, p. 19.

[44] Archives d'Indre-et-Loire, Tours, Série H24, MS No. 3. *Gallia Christiana*, 2, Instrumenta, Col. pp. 366–67.

[45] For what follows see G. Duby, *La société*, pp. 245–60. Robert Boutruche, *Seigneurie et féodalité*, pp. 139–45.

Significantly none of these names ever appeared in records for the Gâtine. For the most part contemporaries continued to resort to the older terms such as *rusticus* and *colonus* mentioned earlier.[46] Only rarely did they acknowledge the changes wrought by the territorial *seigneurie* as when they called peasants *homines consuetudinarii*, or men who were subject to customs.[47] In other words, while revealing that the decisive criterion for distinguishing a peasant from all others was his obligation to pay customs, they seem not to have been overly impressed with the fact. Unless it is due to gaps in the sources the absence of *homini proprii* can only signify that dependence of a personal nature as opposed to dependence through one's land was unusual or unknown in the Gâtine. The *famuli* who made up the *familia* or household of domestic servants of the monks of la Peyratte probably remained in a state of close personal dependence on their lords resembling earlier slavery, but there are only a handful of references to them and they appear to have been very few in number.[48]

Hereditary personal bonds to a lord were unusual but many and probably most peasants were bound to their lands and unable to leave at will. When their land changed hands they remained on it exchanging their former landlord for a new one. Such happened to the *homine rupturario* of one-half a *borderia* belonging to Reginald of Allonne, who acquired a new seigneur when his tenure was donated to the monastery of l'Absie.[49] Likewise, when the lord of Parthenay forbade any of the men of his *domaine* to leave their tenures to move to the newly founded burg of Parthenay-le-Vieux, he did this by virtue of ownership of the land to which they were hereditarily fixed. The same restriction applied to other peasants because they farmed lands on which he had imposed customs, but in neither case did he command them as his personal possessions.[50] Yet in medieval society inability to leave one's land did not by itself constitute serfdom, nor, indeed,

---

[46] See above, p. 102.

[47] ". . . Et quicumque voluerit habitare in ipso burgo, cuiuscumque homo sit, cuiuscumque loci, exceptis nostris dominicis et consuetudinariis hominibus, habitet libere. . . ." Besly, *Histoire*, p. 396. *Chartularium Sancti Jovini*, p. 24. Bibliothèque de Tours, Collection Salmon, MS 1338, p. 262.

[48] *Cartulaire de Talmond*, pp. 171, 173, 174, 176. *Cartulaire de St. Cyprien*, p. 311. Duby, *L'économie rurale*, II, 446–49.

[49] "Reginaudus de Alona . . . dedit dimidiam borderiae terrae quam Caponeria vocatur cum homine rupturario. . . ." *Cartulaires de l'Absie*, p. 88.

[50] For the latin text, see below, p. 122, footnote 76.

had it ever since the time of the *colonus* of the later Roman Empire. People of the eleventh and twelfth centuries were more anxious about establishing an hereditary claim to their land than about securing a theoretical right to leave it.

Completely consistent with the foregoing is the fact that the territorial *seigneurie* does not seem to have been as extensive or as harsh in the Gâtine as elsewhere. A number of customs found in parts of France at that time such as the *chevage*, or head tax, *formariage*, or fine for marrying outside the *seigneurie*, and *droit de gîte*, or obligation to furnish hospitality to the knights and agents of the territorial lord, are never mentioned. Among the others the *corvée* almost certainly made only insignificant demands on the peasantry.[51] Facts like the above leave room for no other conclusion than that the peasants of the Gâtine were not of servile status, or that their servitude to their lords was far more limited than in surrounding regions.

The geography of the region and its relative depopulation in 1000 provide the best explanation for this phenomenon. Inducing colonists to come to a region as poor and unpromising as the Gâtine, especially when it was surrounded by rich plains and plateaux to the south and east, must often have been a trying problem for the local nobility. It is not difficult to imagine that, as others of their class did elsewhere, they enticed peasants to come and settle by offering freedom from some seigneurial exactions and by reducing others in amount.[52]

Although exhibiting certain common traits the members of the peasant class did not form a completely uniform class any more than the nobility. Several quite different elements existed within its ranks. In the first place there was a small peasant aristocracy which in material possessions and prestige was set well apart from the rest of its class. One such man was Geoffrey Airaud, a landholder near the monastery of l'Absie. The first suggestion of his greater landed wealth was his ability to make donations to the monks three or four times in his life as contrasted with the single, deathbed gift of most peasants.[53] From these gifts alone, which,

---

[51] In 1190 the neighboring castellan of Bressuire required only three days a year from the men of his castellany. Belisaire Ledain, *Histoire de Bressuire* (Bressuire, 1880), pp. 265–67. The lord of Parthenay is unlikely to have departed much from this.

[52] Duby, *L'économie rurale*, I, 203–4.

[53] *Cartulaires de l'Absie*, pp. 14, 17, 98, 101.

of course, represented only a part of his total holdings, Geoffrey showed that he had lands at several different places around the monastery, at least one of which was an allod. His peasant status did not prevent him from becoming a landlord over other peasants from whom he collected revenues including the tithe.[54] His wealth and influence quite naturally enabled him to occupy a position of some prominence in the affairs of the parishes of l'Absie and Vernoux. At two formal affairs he mingled with local feudal nobility and on other occasions witnessed the acts of others, including a legal decision handed down by the Lord of Parthenay and his *curia*.[55] The most telling commentary on Geoffrey Airaud is that he can be distinguished from the lower ranks of the nobility only with difficulty.

Equally noteworthy was the ability of a select few peasants to raise themselves well above their class in another way. For the nobility of the Gâtine relied upon peasants to carry out most aspects of seigneurial administration, thus freeing themselves for the activities and life of their own class. Known as *ministri* and *servientes*, both meaning those who serve, these men acquired considerable prestige among their own by escaping at least partially the necessity of tilling the soil, and through being placed in positions of minor command over other peasants. Their principal occupation was with the most menial tasks on the *seigneurie*, those of collecting revenues and rents owed by other tenants. The official who saw that other peasants paid their yearly tithe was the *decimarius*, whereas the *mestivarius* was present when grain crops were harvested to secure his lord's revenues.[56] Posted along the roads of the castellany and at the market places were the *pedagarius* and *vendarius* or two other agents who pocketed the *péage* and *vende*, a circulation and a sales tax.[57] Having quite different duties were the seneschals who were responsible for looking after their lord's household and generally arranging his

---

[54] *Ibid.*, p. 101.

[55] *Ibid.*, pp. 10, 13, 14, 15, 18, 20, 51.

[56] Archives de Maine-et-Loire, Série 101H225 bis, No. 396. MSS Dom Fonteneau, I, 391. *Cartulaires de l'Absie*, p. 81–82.

[57] *Ibid.*, p. 81. L. J. Denis (ed.), *Chartes de St. Julien de Tours*. Archives historiques du Maine (1912–13), pp. 158–59. Among the men of the monks of St. Paul of Parthenay in 1070 was one " Huberto teleonario," or toll collector. *Cartulaire de Cormery*, pp. 90–93.

life at court.[58] But most of these functionaries probably spent most of each year cultivating their lands like everyone else and worked for their lords only intermittently, receiving part of the revenues they collected as payment for their services.

A very few of the *ministri* worked their way to the top of this minor officialdom to become the *prévôts, praepositi,* or chief administrators of a *seigneurie.* The *prévôt* represented his lord in business with others, as for instance, in disputes with the church, besides co-ordinating the activities of all the other agents and acting as the officer of justice on the lands under his command.[59] The pursuit and apprehension of criminals, their trials in the seigneurial court, and the infliction of punishment or amercements all fell to him. As the Lord of Bressuire said around 1090, ". . . my *prévôt* will rectify the wrongs of men. . . ." [60]

The lucrative revenues he received in reward for his work along with his own land doubtless elevated the *prévôt* up among the richest peasants on the *seigneurie.* But it was his power of distraining violators of the law in his *seigneurie* which made the *prévôt* a man respected and feared by both the peasantry and churchmen. The intervention of one Pagan, *prévôt* of Geoffrey Gilbert of Lamairé, in a quarrel between the prior of that place and some local inhabitants needs little commentary. The refusal of the peasants to desist from collecting a tithe which the prior claimed was unjust caused Pagan, with the approval of his lord, to bring together the asses on which they carried the tax, and kill some and cut the ears off others as a warning for the future.[61]

As this incident demonstrates, the *prévôt* derived his superiority

---

[58] Besly, *Histoire,* p. 397. *Cartulaire de Talmond,* p. 174; *Cartulaires de l'Absie,* p. 35.

[59] *Ibid.,* p. 77.

[60] ". . . Prepositus meus injurias hominum rectificabit. . . ." *Chartularium Sancti Jovini,* p. 24. ". . . quod si de ipsa venda, aut aliqua re, in mercato aut in terra domini Parthenaci aut suorum hominum forisfecerit, non distringetur ab ullo ministrorum domini Parthenaci nisi prium. . . ." *Cartulaire de Cormery,* pp. 90–93. ". . . insuper non solum et in istis prenominatis Apostoli Petri terris sed etiam in omnibus prefati cenobi Burguliensis potestatibus vel terris ultra boscum positum nullus ministerialis publicus nec prepositus nec venator . . . neque pro sanguine, pro homicido, pro furtis, pro incendio, pro teloneo . . . introeundi habeant potestatem. . . ." Bibliothèque Nationale, Gaignières, F. L. 17127, pp. 127–28.

[61] ". . . Unde conventi ab eodem monacho et postmodum a domino Gosfrido Gilberti, cum nollent acquiescere, Paganus ipsius prepositus Goffridi, eo jubente, presentibus ipsis, asinos decimam colligentes, alios occidit, aliorum auriculas gladio obtruncavit. . . ." *Cartulaire de Talmond,* p. 293.

over other peasants from the fact that he carried arms and was capable of imposing his will by force. Is it then really surprising to find that early in the twelfth century the *prévôt* of an ecclesiastical *seigneurie*, Emobert Chassan of Foussais, got completely out of hand and domineered over his superiors who were, after all, only unarmed monks. Fed up with his behavior, the prior announced to Emobert that he was depriving him of his office of *prévôt*, only to be told that since that office was hereditary, the monks could not do this. At this the prior was enraged and immediately carried the dispute first to his abbot, the renowned archbishop of Tours, Baudry of Bourgueil, and subsequently to William, count of Poitou, at the latter's court in Poitiers, where Emobert finally relinquished his claims. The scribe then ended the charter by describing how the prior and monks of Foussais then began a custom of making each new *prévôt* swear in the church " with his hand on the altar and in the presence of the parishioners " that he exercised his functions through the consent of the monks and that he claimed no part of it for his patrimony.[62] Many another peasant official must have attempted, as did Emobert, to make his office hereditary, a move which would have solidified his prestigious, but otherwise precarious position. In this instance churchmen triumphantly reaffirmed the old principle of tenure for a lifetime or less, but in many others one suspects they failed.

This same power made easy the transition from seigneurial prévôt to knighthood, the highest position a peasant could reach, and an intermediate class between peasantry and nobility. Some men may have become knights in other ways, but at least two, and probably more, families of the later eleventh century took just such a step.[63] A fuller discussion in an earlier context noted

---

[62] " Ut sciant presentes et futuri quoniam Fousciaci prefectura hereditario jure nulli prevenit manifestum sit quod Emobertus Chassan eiusdem Fusciaci prefectus multa mala per superbiam suam priori suo scilicet Benedicto Godini et aliis monachis ingerebat; unde quadam die inter eos priorem scilicet et Emobertum seditione orta prior monuit Emobertum ne illud amplius prefecturae predictae officium pertracteret; quo audito Emobertus inquit quod per priorem nec per abbatem prefecturam amictere non poterat adjiciens quod hereditario jure sibi contingebat; tunc vero iratus prior Benedictus. . . ." ". . . ex tunc inotescuit consuetudo ut quicque Fusciaci prefecturae regimen susciperet supra altare manu imposita coram populo jurare ne eam ultra abbatis et monachorum libitum teneret et ne in ea hereditatis suae aliquid ascriberet." Bibliothèque de Tours, Collection Salmon, MS 1338, p. 406.

[63] See above, p. 94, footnote 79.

that their power made some of the knights of the region almost indistinguishable from the nobility and, indeed, probably led to their gradual assimilation into that class.[64] If peasants of the eleventh and twelfth centuries had any access at all to the nobility surely it was through knighthood.

Another small group of peasants who benefited from a status superior to the rest of their class, but whose exact identity is obscure were the *clientes*, or clients. A charter of Thibaud of Beaumont around 1090 demonstrates that the *clientes* were a kind of elite who were exempt from the customs paid by other peasants, but aside from this it is difficult to ascertain the exact nature of their relationship to their lord or whether they had any specific tasks to perform. Some of Thibaud's *clientes* who were engaged in buying and selling in the market of Chiché were apparently abusing certain market privileges which they enjoyed, for he issued a warning that if any one of them paid interest on a purchase he would become a *homo consuetudinarius*, one subject to seigneurial customs, like other peasants.[65] In the later eleventh century the lord of l'Absie had a *cliens,* Audouin Abhorret, who ran errands for him as a kind of personal servant.[66] At least once the title *cliens* seems to have been the equivalent of vassal, for Petronius of St. Hilaire-de-Voust, *cliens* of Jean Gestins of Vouvant, was an influential man who had land of his own, received revenues from other peasants, and on one occasion was present at a feudal assembly of a great Poitevin baron, Geoffrey Rancon, lord of Vouvant.[67] Two other *clientes* seem to have been nothing more than holders of peasant tenures.[68] Left with nothing more than this, one can only assert that the *clientes* were privileged in one sense but still closely dependent on their lords.[69]

[64] See above, pp. 91–96.

[65] ". . . clientes meos proprios retineo, et monachi proprios habeant suos. Si autem mei vel sui ad lucrum emerint, sint consuetudinarii sicut alii. . . ." *Chartularium Sancti Jovini,* p. 24.

[66] ". . . quinimo responderunt sibi veteres coloni . . . quod Audoinus Abhorret cliens Jacquelini qui fuerat dominus ecclesiae Absiae . . . referebat de Capella Seguini et de Vernol offerturam ad dominum suum Jacquelinum, propter parochiatum ecclesiae Absiae. . . ." *Cartulaires de l'Absie,* p. 7.

[67] *Cartulaires de l'Absie,* pp. 6, 98, 102.

[68] ". . . teste; Bernardo cliente ejusdem terre. . . ." *Ibid.,* pp. 37, 103.

[69] Henri Dubled reached a similar conclusion regarding the *clientes* in Alsace. Dubled, "Cliens," *Revue du moyen âge latin* (1950), pp. 317–19.

Alongside the farmers and various seigneurial officials came the last important segment of the peasantry, the burgers, or the inhabitants of the burgs. It will be recalled that settlers built these communities, a dozen or more in number, as part of the colonization movement of the later eleventh century, that some were in rural areas and others outside castles, and that in appearance they resembled the ordinary rural villages of houses and a church, except for some sort of enclosing fence.[70] Detailed charters on the burgs of St. Paul of Parthenay, Parthenay-le-Vieux, Secondigny, and Chiché show that the main difference between the two types of settlement rested in the freedom of the inhabitants of the burgs from the territorial *seigneurie*. When the founder, invariably a nobleman, established the burg, he surrendered to its monastic owners his right to collect customs of any kind in the burg and on its land, a sweeping concession of considerable importance.[71] Insofar as markets were concerned it was specified that no sales taxes, highway taxes, or taxes for displaying one's goods in booths would be taken from the local burgers.[72] From now on the market was in the hands of the monks to whom the burg had been given and who had officials of their own to police it.[73] In addition the secular lord abandoned his rights of justice over the burgers to their monastic lord.[74] The lord of Parthenay made a further concession to the burgers of Parthenay-le-Vieux and St. Paul of Parthenay when he exempted those who left the burg to sell their goods at markets and fairs in his castle from both his road tax and justice while en route.[75] Finally he invited

---

[70] See above, pp. 26–28.

[71] ". . . Simon vero de Parthenaco dedit Deo et St. Paulo . . . omnes consuetudines de burgo Sancti Pauli, ut nec ipse nec quicumque Parthenacum tenuerit, ullam consuetudinem in burgo nec in terra Sti Pauli, nec teloneum, nec paedagium nec prehensionem, nec bidamnum, nec credentiam, nec ullam insuper omino consuetudinem. . . ." *Cartulaire de Cormery*, pp. 90–93.

[72] *Ibid.*

[73] The seigneurial agents for the monks of St. Paul in 1070 included a toll collector, a mayor, and a marshal. *Ibid.*

[74] ". . . Quod si aliquid eorum aliquid admiserit contra Principem Castri seu adversum quemquam suorum, non dijudicabitur ab ullo nisi monachorum judicio. . . ." Bibliothèque Nationale, Gaignières, F. L. 17127, p. 379.

[75] ". . . Nullus homo habitans in terra Sancti Pauli, veniens ad mercatum vel rediens a mercate, dabit ullam consuetudinem, nisi juxta mendam (sic for *vendam*) in mercato domini Parthenaci . . . Si quis homo habitans in terra St. Pauli minaverit, vel portaverit vel adminaverit, vel apportaverit aliquid foras ad mercatum, vel aliquam feriam, nec in eundo, nec in redeundo, ullum pedagium dabit domino Parthenaci . . .," *Cartulaire de Cormery*, pp. 90–93.

men not subject to his authority to come and settle in the new burgs and promised them protection from their former lords, should the latter attempt to force them back to their old lands.[76]

At first glance the impression arises that these proclamations created a new class in society, one singled out from the rest through its immunity to certain market taxes and secular seigneurial jurisdiction, and through its peculiar way of life, namely, a preoccupation with buying and selling. For the most part, this impression is false. In the first place, the franchises did not release the burgers from all customs and jurisdiction whatsoever, they merely transferred the authority to collect them from the lord of Parthenay to the head of the monastic community. It was the monks who benefitted, whereas the burgers simply acquired a new lord to whom to pay their taxes. Only if the rule of their monastic lords was more lenient than that of the lay donor, and it probably was in order to attract newcomers, would the burgers have differed from other peasants in the Gâtine. In any case the difference cannot have been great or men would have drawn a sharper line between the two classes than they did.

To assume also that the burgers of the region were a class of traders and merchants would be a grave mistake, for the Gâtine was a remote rural area and little touched by inter-regional trade. Burgs like Boismé, Breuil Bernard, Allonne, and Lamairé must have been important commercially only in serving as markets in agricultural produce at a parish level, but very little survives to record activity even on that small scale.[77] Their inhabitants probably traded at the markets which most burgs had, but most of them must have worked the soil for a living just like other peasants. In the light of the resultant similarity between peasants and most burgers it is quite understandable that contemporaries very seldom used the term *burgenses* to describe the inhabitants of a burg, but more often had recourse to vague and general words like *habitatores* and *homines habitentes*, inhabitants, or simply

[76] ". . . Et quicumque voluerit habitare in ipso burgo (Parthenay-le-Vieux), cuiuscumque homo sit, cuiuscumque loci, exceptis nostris dominicis et consuetudinariis hominibus, habitet libere, sicut et alii defendendus et protegendus, a nullo hominum disturbium patiendus, seu requisitione alicuius numquam ab inde removendus, aut aliquod iniuriae vel contrarietatis, ibi aut alicube perpessurus. . . ." Besly, *Histoire*, p. 396.

[77] Rye was bought and sold publicly in the market of Lamairé around 1100. ". . . qua publice venditur et emitur. . . ." *Cartulaire de Talmond*, p. 175.

called them the men of the prior, titles which could be applied equally well to peasants.[78] Indeed, the wording of one charter shows that newly arriving burgers were treated as *hospites*, or settlers, men who cleared land and put it under cultivation.[79] Many seigneurs may have viewed the burg primarily as a means of getting land settled quickly and efficiently.

Nonetheless, burgers in and around Parthenay constituted an important exception. Some of those who brought their goods to the castle to sell were undoubtedly among the artisans making the woolen cloths for which Parthenay was known.[80] One reads also of other craftsmen and retailers such as the blacksmith and baker, and in the later twelfth century, of a physician, " Petrus medicus de Parteniaco." [81] One other type of burger in both Secondigny and Parthenay deserves to be mentioned because of the special tasks he carried out. This was the urban agent of the Cistercian monastery of l'Absie and of the Grandmontain priory of Bois d'Allonne. The monastic rules of both of those orders specified that their houses be isolated in the countryside and forbade them to have establishments or priories in towns.[82] Thus to enable them to have permanent access to a market, the lord of Parthenay asigned each of them a burger both in Parthenay and Secondigny who acted as a general purchasing agent and as such was free from all service and customs, including the usual sales and highway taxes.[83] This kind of man, and not the majority

---

[78] *Cartulaire de Cormery*, pp. 90–93. Besly, *Histoire*, p. 396. The first reference to a *burgens* occurred in 1169 when William III of Parthenay spoke of " unum burgensem apud Secondiniacum. . . ." *Cartulaires de l'Absie*, p. 81.

[79] See above, p. 29, footnote 37.

[80] Very little is known about the woolen industry of Parthenay except that it reached out beyond the Gâtine to link the region with adjoining provinces. A document of 1097 from the Saintonge, fifty miles to the south, mentions some " so-called cloths of Parthenay," and later in the twelfth century some of the same fabrics were taxed when crossing the Loire river, seventy miles north of the town. ". . . Quinque ulnas de panno qui dicitur de Partiniaco . . .." *Cartulaire de St. Jean d'Angély*, I, 150. ". . . 4 denarii pro trosello de panis Partiniace . . .." *Layettes du Trésor des chartes*, I, 117.

[81] *Cartulaires de l'Absie*, p. 81. *Cartulaire de Talmond*, p. 175. Archives de Maine-et-Loire, Série 231H1, Domaine de Vallette, No. 1.

[82] The dependence of the monks of Bois d'Allonne on outsiders was absolute since they could own no land except that on which their house was built and relied on visitors and benefactors like the lord of Parthenay for all of their food. Dom Jean Becquet, " La règle de Grandmont," *Bulletin de la société archéologique et historique du Limousin* (1958), pp. 16 ff.

[83] MSS Dom Fonteneau, I, 391–93. *Cartulaires de l'Absie*, pp. 5, 81.

of the burgers, did indeed form a special element within the peasantry. Immersed in the atmosphere of town life and occasionally exposed to the world beyond the Gâtine through their travels, they not only led another kind of life from their fellows but must also have had a vastly different outlook on it.

CONCLUSION

The end of the twelfth century is a useful terminal date in the history of the medieval Gâtine for several reasons. By that time the broad outlines of the settlement of the region, which had once been a wilderness of woods, underbrush, and abandoned habitations, had become unmistakably visible and were not to change radically until about a century ago. Almost all of the present day villages had been occupied, the major castles and parish churches had been built, and Parthenay had emerged as the one real center of population by then. Moreover, the countryside had already begun to look as it does today with many widely dispersed settlements of small dimensions, most with their arable fields and pastures clearly delimited by surrounding ditches and high hedges. As this pattern tends to indicate, the Gâtine was a region with an essentially rural economy of agriculture and livestock, and with only a trickle of trade in its capital at Parthenay.

These two centuries are also highly important from one other point of view, for they saw the rise of the noble house of Parthenay and the maturing of feudal government under its direction. Ever since the middle decades of the eleventh century, the lords of Parthenay had been sovereign rulers of most of the Gâtine, commanding feudal allegiances from the nobility of the region and exacting seigneurial customs and taxes from the peasantry. The years around 1200 did not bring any sudden or drastic changes in the history of that family, such as ending its independence, but the presence of King John of England in Parthenay did herald things to come. Having seen its territorial expansion checked by disastrous wars with the counts of Anjou and Poitou early in the twelfth century, the lords of Parthenay now witnessed the first of a series of invasions of the region by contending kings of England and France which would almost inevitably result in the compromise of that independence.

It was during the eleventh and twelfth centuries that the

125

medieval society of the Gâtine acquired the form which it retained for hundreds of years afterward. In a position of dominance was an elite, or nobility, which, under its principal representative, the lord of Parthenay, ruled the entire region. Ownership of most of the land in the Gâtine and control over the peasants working it enabled noblemen to regulate most of the economic life of the region. The principle of membership through heredity protected the immunities and privileges of this class. More numerous than the nobility, but still a minority of the total population, was the clergy, a class of varied composition, but of unquestioned prestige and wealth. The clergy of the Gâtine, which has not been discussed in detail in this study, included common parish priests or men of peasant origin, as well as abbots and an archpriest in Parthenay, men who were normally of noble families. Their possession of some of the largest *seigneuries* in the region and the steady influx of pious donations which enlarged those estates, gave the monks of the Gâtine, who represented at least ten different monasteries, enormous economic power in addition to their religious authority. Making up the great mass of society were peasants who farmed land which in most cases they rented from the nobility. The peasantry was a class of some complexity, ranging all the way from simple farmers to agricultural administrators, to armed knights, and to artisans and a few traders. Resting on most peasants was the obligation to pay rent and taxes to one or more lords, but these were generally reduced in severity, whereas the more onerous and hated forms of servitude common to western Europe at that time were totally absent from the region.

In all of these developments the society of the Gâtine revealed few striking or novel characteristics when compared with the society of other parts of France at that time. Its movement of colonization was more intensive due to previous depopulation, but its scattered settlements, its partially enclosed fields, its rural economy, and its meager population plainly associated it with adjoining regions in the western part of the country. The imposition of personal government by regional castellans through fiefs and dependent relationships occurred at approximately the same time in many other places although the feudal bond in the Gâtine was probably less extensive and less restrictive. Its noble class enjoyed the same privileged status as other nobilities, and seems to have differed only in being proportionately smaller in size, in drawing a clearer line between noblemen and knights, and in following a highly unusual system of inheritance. If any segment of society departed significantly from prevailing patterns or trends, it was the peasantry. The *seigneurie* was firmly implanted in the region, perhaps even more firmly than in other parts of western France, but it weighed less heavily on the peasant class than it did elsewhere. The need for settlers in an unattractive region doubtless accounted for the absence of most forms of serfdom. Thus this, like the other distinctive traits of the society of the eleventh and twelfth centuries, derived in large part from the nature of the region and the circumstances under which it was settled.

The history of this two-century period is not a particularly exciting or dramatic one except from the viewpoint of its own inhabitants. For them it must have been a period of turbulence with their normal life being interrupted periodically by feudal wars which, although local in importance were, nonetheless, destructive. Yet there are also indications that the Gâtine bene-fited from enough peace in the twelfth century to permit artistic activity of more than one kind. This is the great period of church building in the Gâtine, and a large number of the original edifices are still the landmarks of their modern villages. Many are quite simple and undeserving of much attention, but some like Champ-deniers and Fenioux are beautiful examples of Romanesque archi-tecture, the style which flourished in twelfth-century Poitou. Particularly noteworthy also are the sculptured figures of horsemen and pedestrians on the façade of the magnificent, and now aban-doned, church of Parthenay-le-Vieux, the mausoleum of the lords of Parthenay. Almost as impressive and just as utilitarian as the Romanesque churches are a few stately bridges of the same style which stand in out-of-the-way corners of the Gâtine and which, along with the ruined castle of Parthenay, are among the only examples of secular architecture still extant today. Interestingly enough the Gâtine also boasts a literary figure in the twelfth century. Aimery Picaud, a canon of Parthenay, was the author of a famous guidebook for pilgrims making the journey to St. James of Compostella in Spain.[1]

---

[1] Jeanne Vieilliard (ed.), *Le guide du Pèlèrin de Saint-Jacques de Compostelle. Texte latin du XIIᵉ siècle, édité et traduit en Français d'après les manuscrits de Compostelle et de Ripoll* (2nd edition, Macon, 1950).

On the whole, the history of the Gâtine during the eleventh and twelfth centuries is not one distinguished by great men and striking events. Nevertheless, it is important in the less spectacular but more lasting sense that the foundations of an entire society were then laid.

APPENDIX

The Origin of the Family of Parthenay.

The conclusion that the first lord of Parthenay came either from Anjou or the Touraine hinges first on the extent of the feudal holdings in Poitou of the count of Anjou. As the result of war in the later tenth century between the counts of Anjou and Poitou, the former, Geoffrey Grisgonelle, accepted high tracts of land in northern Poitou as fiefs from his rival.[1] In consequence a large tongue of land stretching from the Loire in a southerly direction through Loudun, Moncontour, and Mirebeau and touching the environs of Poitiers on the east was dependent on the count of Anjou.[2] In the past historians have placed the boundary between Poitou and Anjou to the north and east of the Gâtine by some ten to fifteen miles.[3] But for the later tenth and eleventh centuries either this line should be placed further south to include large parts or most of the Gâtine, or, if that region was not Angevin, then the count of Anjou at least held sizable fiefs there. Partial proof is offered by a royal charter of the year 973 or 975 whereby the king of France, Lothaire, approved a gift of the Count of Anjou to the convent of St. Jean of Bonnevalle near

[1] ". . . Eodem tempore gravissimum bellum inter Guillelmum ducem et Gosfridum Andegavensem comitem, peractus est. Sed Gosfridus necessitatibus actus, Guillelmo duci se subdidit, seque ei in manibus praebuit, et ab eo castrum Losdunum cum nonnullis aliis in pago Pictavorum pro beneficio accepit. . ." Ademar de Chabannes, *Chronique.* Jules Chavanon, ed., Collection de textes pour servir à l'étude et à l'enseignement de l'histoire (Paris, 1897), p. 152.

[2] When Fulk Nerra succeeded his father Geoffrey Grisgonelle as count of Anjou in 987 he received, in addition to fiefs in the Loudunais, the city of Saintes, and a number of castles in the Saintonge from the count of Poitou. ". . . Cumque comitem andegavensem, fulchonem, in manibus suis commendatum haberet, concesserat ei pro beneficio Losdunum cum aliis nonnullis castris in pictavorum solo, sanctonas quoque cum quibusdam castellis . . .," *ibid.,* p. 164.

[3] See Ledain, *Dictionaire,* under *Marche commune,* p. 169; J. Boussard, *Le comté d'Anjou sous Henri Plantagenêt et ses fils (1151–1204).* Bibliothèque de l'École des Hautes Études, 1938, Fasc. 271, p. 19; L. Halphen, *Le comté d'Anjou au XIe siècle* (Paris, 1906), p. 54.

Thouars of three churches, including one in the northern Gâtine, Faye-l'Abbesse, and another just outside St. Maixent to the south.[4] All three were held in fief from the count of Poitou. Moreover Fulk Nerra of Anjou witnessed three early eleventh-century acts of Count William the Great concerning lands which the latter held in the western and southern parts of the Gâtine.[5] His presence on those occasions could hardly have been a coincidence. It is much more probable that he attended those donations as an interested vassal who possessed lands adjoining those of his feudal suzerain. Another indication that Angevin authority extended much farther south than has been suspected up until now comes from the *Conventum* of about 1020, where Hugh of Lusignan, a feudal baron from southeast of the Gâtine, tells that he had recently been a vassal of the Count of Anjou.[6] Further evidence is furnished by the fact that one of the leading castellans of Anjou, the lord of Montreuil-Bellay, had extensive estates in the Gâtine and frequently visited the region in the eleventh and twelfth centuries.[7] In the twelfth century a member of one of the two leading families of Secondigny was one Gautier of Anjou, and it is noteworthy that the money in circulation in the Gâtine at that time was almost always Angevin.[8] The argument draws added strength from the close association of the lords of Parthenay with the house of Anjou all through the eleventh and early twelfth centuries. When he died Joscelin of Parthenay was a vassal of Fulk Nerra for his castle and the lords of Parthenay nearly always supported the Angevin cause in the frequent wars between the counts of Anjou and Poitou. Moreover it is striking that distant monasteries in Anjou and the Touraine such as Cormery, St. Julien

[4] Louis Halphen, Ferdinand Lot (eds.), *Recueil des actes de Lothaire et de Louis V, rois de France, 954–987* (Paris, 1908), pp. 145–49. This act in its present form did not issue directly from the royal chancery but its contents are so obviously genuine and contemporary to the events which they describe that Halphen and Lot have surmised that it was rewritten with very few changes in the eleventh century.

[5] On those three occasions the count of Poitou made gifts of land at Brettignolles (1004), St. Paul-en-Gâtine (1017), and Vouvant (1010–21). Bibliothèque Nationale, Gaignières, F. L. 17127, pp. 127–28. Besly, *Histoire*, p. 307. *Gallia Christiani*, 11, Instrumenta, Col. 330.

[6] J. Besly, *Histoire*, p. 291.

[7] *Cartulaires de l'Absie*, pp. 22, 27, 88; Archives de la Haute-Loire, 1H185, Nos. 2 and 3.

[8] *Cartulaires de l'Absie*, pp. 18, 21, 22, 27, 30, 31, 34, 54, 73, 74, 111.

of Tours, St. Florent of Saumur, Fontevrault and Bourgueil bene-
fited more often from the liberality of the lords of Parthenay than
did the neighboring institutions of Poitou. And on a significant
number of occasions they witnessed the acts of other Angevin
nobility in various parts of that country. Such actions are best
explained by presuming that the founder of the line came originally from either Anjou or the Touraine and continued to maintain
close connections there.

Still more support for this theory comes from a consideration
of the origins of the castle which in Parthenay, as in other places
in Poitou, seems to have furnished the foundation for a noble
dynasty. There is no reason to believe that Parthenay castle dates
from much before 1012 when first mentioned, especially since
many other Poitevin castles stem from the same period. The
construction of a castle, particularly the massive stone edifices of
the late tenth century and thereafter, frequently caught the attention of medieval chroniclers who took pains to note the event
and it is unlikely that any escaped mention for long. Fulk Nerra
of Anjou is known to have fortified other of his Poitevin fiefs
such as Montcontour and Mirebeau around 1000, and he could
well have built Parthenay castle at the same time.[9] Viewed
separately, none of the above facts proves anything, but viewed
together they strongly suggest that the Parthenay family, from
either Anjou or the Touraine, received the castle and some of the
Gâtine as a fief from the count of Anjou around the year 1000.

To adopt this explanation means rejecting the version apparently
first proposed by Paul Marchegay around 1845 and taken over
with no change by succeeding historians.[10] Marchegay, considering
the extensive land holdings of the lords of Parthenay in the early
eleventh century, contended that the family must have gone back
well into the ninth century since such *domaines* could not have
been acquired over a short period of time.[11] Charters from the
eleventh century demonstrate that the family held lands from
far-spread parts of Bas Poitou in fief from the count of Poitou
and the viscount of Thouars. But these could hardly have been

[9] S. Painter, *Castellans of the Plain of Poitou*, p. 248.
[10] Paul Marchegay, *Notice sur les archevêques, ancien seigneurs de Parthenay*, no
date or place of publication. A copy is to be found in the Bibliothèque Municipale
of Poitiers.
[11] *Ibid.*, p. 151.

obtained in the ninth or even the greater part of the tenth century since during that time Bas Poitou was the primary target for Norse raids which left it unpopulated for over a century and a half. Recolonization did not begin there until early in the eleventh century. Alfred Richard made a pertinent suggestion as to the manner in which both the lords of Parthenay and the viscounts of Thouars could have amassed their vast properties there. By a treaty concluded sometime after 981 William Fier-a-bras, count of Poitou, and Guerech, count of Nantes, divided up western Bas Poitou among themselves with the former keeping the southern part of that region. Richard proposed that Count William then assigned much of his portion in fief to the Viscount of Thouars and the Lord of Parthenay.[12] This explains furthermore why the Count of Poitou as well as the Count of Anjou had rights of wardship over the family and posessions of the deceased Joscelin early in the eleventh century.

[12] Richard, *Histoire des comtes de Poitou*, I, 174, footnote 2.

BIBLIOGRAPHY

This study is based almost exclusively on ecclesiastical records, the archives of the various monasteries which owned either land or dependent religious houses in the Gâtine. Although many acts still exist in their original form, most of them survive as they were preserved by contemporaries in a somewhat condensed or abridged form in collected volumes known as cartularies.

UNPUBLISHED SOURCE MATERIALS

Most of the monastic archives of eleventh- and twelfth-century Poitou have already been published, but two notable exceptions are the extremely important cartularies and scores of individual acts of the monasteries of Fontevrault (Maine-et-Loire) and Bourgueil (Indre-et-Loire), both about seventy miles north of the Gâtine.

ABBEY OF FONTEVRAULT:

About one-third of the original cartulary of Fontevrault still exists in two separate parts, one at the Bibliothèque Nationale in Paris, and another in the Departmental Archives at Angers (Maine-et-Loire).

1. Archives de Maine-et-Loire, Série 101H225, *Pancarta et Cartularium Fontis Ebraudi.*

2. Bibliothèque Nationale, Nouvelles acquisitions 2414, *Pancarta et Cartularium Fontis Ebraudi.*

3. Archives de Maine-et-Loire, Série 101H225 bis, *L'abbaye de Fontevrault; extrait des cartulaires, chartes, obituaires, registres.* This seventeenth-century copy, taken from the original, enables one to fill in some of the gaps in the missing two-thirds of the original cartulary.

4. Bibliothèque Nationale, Collection Gaignières, F. L. 5480, *L'abbaye de Fontevrault.* This is an early eighteenth-century collection of incomplete extracts made from the cartulary.

5. Archives de Maine-et-Loire, *Fonds de Fontevrault*, Série 231H1, Prieuré de Valettes; and Série 187H1, Prieuré de Montibeuf. These are collections of original charters of the twelfth century.

ABBEY OF BOURGUEIL:

1. *Extrait du cartulaire de l'abbaye de Bourgueil.* In the private possession of M. Goupil de Bouillé of Pavée, Bourgueil (Indre-et-Loire), this copy of 1719 is the oldest and most complete copy of an older cartulary of 1481. Unfortunately M. de Bouillé, while most graciously allowing people to consult his cartulary at his chateau of Pavée, has steadfastly resisted attempts to have it microfilmed and made available to more scholars.

133

2. Bibliothèque de la ville de Tours. Collection of André Salmon, MSS 1338, 1339, *Abbaye de Bourgueil: recueil de titres relatifs à l'abbaye de Bourgueil ou essai de reconstitution d'un ancien cartulaire*. Based largely on the preceding cartulary this highly valuable compilation also incorporates some original charters not included there.

3. Bibliothèque Nationale, Collection Gaignières, F. L. 17127, *Abbaye de Bourgueil*. An incomplete collection of abridged charters made in the early eighteenth century.

4. Archives d'Indre-et-Loire, Série H24, *Abbaye de Bourgueil*, 18 pièces parchemins (990–1086). Original charters.

ARCHIVES DE LA VIENNE, Série H, *Abbaye de Fontaine-le-Comte*, Carton 6, No. 7. Original charters relating to the priory of Bois de Secondigny in the Gâtine.

ARCHIVES DE LA HAUTE-LOIRE, Séries H184, Nos. 1–3, and Série H185, Nos. 1–4, *Abbaye de la Chaise-Dieu*. Original charters of the priory of Parthenay-le-Vieux.

BIBLIOTHÈQUE DE LA VILLE DE POITIERS, Dom Fonteneau: *Les mémoires ou le recueil de diplômes, chartes, notices et autres actes authentiques pour servir à l'histoire du Poitou . . . etc.*, 87 volumes. As preparation for a large-scale history of the counts of Poitou this eighteenth-century Benedictine made copies of most of the great monastic cartularies in the province. Since many archives were then destroyed in the French Revolution, this is an invaluable collection of source materials for medieval Poitou.

PUBLISHED SOURCE MATERIALS

Those records which were consulted only once or twice have not been included in this list of basic sources, having been cited in footnotes at the appropriate points in the text.

BESLY, JEAN, *Histoire des comtes de Poictou et des ducs de Guyenne, contenant ce qui s'est passé de plus mémorable en France depuis l'an, 811, jusques au Roy Louis le Jeune*. Paris, 1647. The earliest scholar to undertake a history of the entire province of Poitou, Besly included in his *Preuves* a large number of documents which have since disappeared or are not yet published.

Cartulaires et chartes de l'abbaye de l'Absie, ed. BELISAIRE LEDAIN. Archives historiques du Poitou, T 25.

Cartulaire de l'abbaye royale de Notre-Dame des Châtelliers, ed. LOUIS DUVAL. Mémoires de la société de statistique des Deux-Sèvres, 1872.

Cartulaire de Cormery précédé de l'histoire de l'abbaye et de la ville de Cormery, ed. J. BOURASSÉ. Mémoires de la société archéologique de Touraine, 1861.

Cartulaire de l'abbaye de St. Cyprien de Poitiers, ed. LOUIS REDET. Archives historiques du Poitou, T 3.

Cartulaire de Saint-Jean d'Angély, ed. GEORGES MUSSET. Archives historiques de la Saintonge et de l'Aunis, 1901.

Cartulaire du Prieuré de Saint-Nicolas de Poitiers, ed. LOUIS REDET. Archives historiques du Poitou, T 1.

Cartulaire de l'abbaye royale de Notre-Dame de Saintes, ed. L'ABBÉ GRASILIER in *Cartulaires inédits de la Saintonge*. Niort, 1871.

Cartulaire de l'abbaye de Saint-Croix-de-Talmond, ed. LOUIS DE LA BOUTETIÈRE. Mémoires de la société des antiquaires de l'ouest, 1872.

PAUL MARCHEGAY (ed.). *Cartulaires du Bas-Poitou*. Les Roches-Baritaud, 1877.

Chartes poitevines de l'abbaye de Saint-Florent, près de Saumur, ed. PAUL MARCHE-GAY. Archives historiques du Poitou, 1872.

Chartes de l'abbaye de Nouaillé, ed. DOM P. DE MONSABERT. Archives historiques du Poitou, T 49.

Chartes et documents pour servir à l'histoire de l'abbaye de St. Maixent, ed. ALFRED RICHARD. Archives historiques du Poitou, T 16, T 18.

Chartes inédites de l'abbaye de St. Croix de Poitiers, ed. DOM P. DE MONSABERT. Revue Mabillon, 1913–14.

Chroniques des églises d'Anjou, ed. P. MARCHEGAY and ÉMILE MABILLE. Société de l'histoire de France, 1860.

Chroniques des comtes d'Anjou, ed. P. MARCHEGAY and ANDRÉ SALMON. Société de l'histoire de France, 1856–71.

Chartularium Sancti Jovini, ed. C. GRANDMAISON. Mémoires de la société de statistique des Deux-Sèvres, 1854.

Documents pour servir à l'histoire de l'église de St. Hilaire de Poitiers, ed. LOUIS REDET. Mémoires de la société des antiquaires de l'ouest, 1847, 1852.

Gallia Christiana, Parisis, 1715–1865, Tome 2.

H. BEAUCHET-FILLEAU (ed). *Pouillé du diocèse de Poitiers*. Niort, 1868.

SECONDARY LITERATURE

BECQUET, DOM JEAN. "La règle de Grandmont," *Bulletin de la société archéologique et historique du Limousin*, 1958.

BLOCH, MARC. *La société féodale; la formation des liens de dépendence; les classes et le gouvernement des hommes*. 2 vols. Paris, 1949.

———. *Les caractères originaux de l'histoire rurale française*, Nouvelle édition, 2 vols. Paris, 1955.

BOBIN, ROBERT. *La Gâtine: étude de géographie*. Niort, 1926.

BONENFANT, P. and G. DESPY. "La noblesse en Brabant (XII–XIII siècles); quelques sondages," *Le Moyen Age*, 1958.

BOUSSARD, JACQUES. "La vie en Anjou aux XIe et XIIe siècles," *Le Moyen Age*, 1950.

———. "Le Comté de Mortain au XIe siècle," *Le Moyen Age*, 1953.

———. *Le gouvernment d'Henri II Plantagenêt*, Paris, 1956.

———. "L'origine des familles seigneuriales dans la région de la Loire moyenne," *Cahiers de civilisation médiévale*, 1962.

———. "Aspects particulières de la féodalité dans l'Empire Plantagenêt," *Bulletin de la société des antiquaires de l'ouest*, 1963.

BOUTERON, MARCEL. "Guillaume l'archevêque," *Mélanges Bémont* (Paris, 1913), pp. 139–41.

BOUTRUCHE, ROBERT. *Une société provinciale en lutte contre la féodalité; l'Alleu en Bordelais et en Bazadais du XIe au XVIIIe siècle*. Publications de la faculté des lettres de l'Université de Strasbourg, 100. Rodez, 1942.

———. *Seigneurie et féodalité, I, le premier âge des liens d'homme à homme*. Collection historique. Paris, 1959.

CHAPUIS, M. "La noblesse dans le pays de Vaud aux XIe et XIIe siècles," *Mémoires de la société pour l'histoire du droit et des institutions des anciens pays bourguignons, comtois et romands*, 1948–49.

CHÉDEVILLE, A. "Étude de la mise en valeur et du peuplement du Maine au XIe siècle d'après les documents de l'abbaye de St. Vincent du Mans," *Annales de Bretagne*, 1960.

CROZET, RENÉ. *L'art Roman en Poitou*. Poitiers, 1949.

DÉLÉAGE, ANDRÉ, *La vie rurale en Bourgogne jusqu'au début du onzième siècle*. 3 vols. Macon, 1941.

DOLLINGER, PHILLIPE. *L'évolution des classes rurales en Bavière*. Publications de la faculté des lettres de l'Université de Strasbourg, 112. Paris, 1949.

DUBLED, HENRI. "Quelques observations sur le sens du mot *villa*," *Le Moyen Age*, 1953.

———. "Noblesse et féodalité en Alsace du XIe au XIIIe siècle," *Tijdschrift vor Rechtsgeschiedenis*, 1960.

DUBY, GEORGES. *L'économie rurale et la vie des campagnes dans l'occident médiéval (France, Angleterre, Empire, IXe–XVe siècles). Essai de synthèse et perspectives de recherches*. Collection historique, 2 vols. Paris, 1962.

———. *La société aux XIe et XIIe siècles dans la région Maconnaise*. Bibliothèque générale de l'école pratique des hautes études, VIe section. Paris, 1953.

———. "Une enquête à poursuivre; la noblesse dans la France médiévale," *Revue Historique*, 1961.

DUPONT, ANDRÉ. "Considerations sur la colonisation et la vie rurale dans le Roussillon et la marche d'Espagne au IXe siècle," *Annales du Midi*, 1955.

FOURNIER, G. "La seigneurie en basse-Auvergne aux XIe et XIIe siècles d'après les censives du cartulaire de Sauxillanges," *Mélanges d'histoire du moyen âge dédiés à la mémoire de Louis Halphen*. Paris, 1951.

GANSHOF, F. L. *Feudalism*. Translated by PHILIP GRIERSON. (2nd English ed.) New York, 1961.

GARAUD, MARCEL. *Essai sur les institutions judiciares du Poitou*. Poitiers, 1910.

———. *L'abbaye de Sainte-Croix de Talmond en Bas-Poitou, ca. 1049–1250 d'après le cartulaire; étude d'histoire économique et sur le droit du Poitou au moyen âge*. Poitiers, 1914.

———. "Le viage ou le retour du vieux coustumier de Poitou," *Bulletin de la société des antiquaires de l'ouest*, 1921.

———. "Les vicomtes de Poitou (IXe–XIIe siècles)," *Revue historique de droit français et étranger*, 1937.

———. "Les incursions des normands en Poitou et leurs conséquences," *Revue historique* (1937).

———. "Les origines des *pagi* poitevins au moyen âge. VIe–XIe siècle," *Revue historique de droit français et étranger*, 1949.

———. "L'organisation administrative du comté de Poitou au 10e siècle et l'avènement des châtelains et des châtellenies," *Bulletin de la société des antiquaires de l'ouest*, 1953.

GENICOT, LÉOPOLD. "La noblesse au moyen âge dans l'ancien *Francie*," *Annales, économies, sociétés, civilisations*, 1962.

———. *L'économie rurale Namuroise au bas moyen âge*. Vol. 2, *Les hommes, la noblesse*. Recueil de travaux d'histoire et de philologie de l'Université de Louvain, 4th Series, 20th fascicule.

———. *L'économie rurale Namuroise au bas moyen âge*, Vol. I, *La seigneurie foncière*. Recueil de travaux d'histoire et de philologie de l'Université de Louvain, 3rd series, 17th fascicule.

GRAND, ROGER and RAYMOND DELATOUCHE. *L'agriculture au moyen âge de la fin de l'empire romain au XVe siècle*. L'agriculture à travers les âges, III. Paris, 1950.

HALPHEN, LOUIS. "La justice en France au moyen âge," *A travers l'histoire du moyen âge* (1950), pp. 175–202.

———. *Le Comté d'Anjou au XIe siècle*. Paris, 1906.

HIGOUNET, CHARLES. "Observations sur la seigneurie rurale et l'habitat en Rouergue du IXᵉ au XIVᵉ siècle," *Annales du Midi*, 1950.

IMBERT, HUGHES. "Notice sur les vicomtes de Thouars de la famille de ce nom," *Mémoires de la société des antiquaires de l'ouest*, 1864.

LATOUCHE, ROBERT. "Un aspect de la vie rurale dans le Maine au XIᵉ et au XIIᵉ siècle: l'établissement des bourgs," *Le Moyen Age*, 1937.

————. "Défrichement et peuplement rural dans le Maine du IXᵉ au XIIIᵉ siècle," *Le Moyen Age* (1948), pp. 77–87.

————. *Les origines de l'économie occidentale; IVᵉ au XIᵉ siècle.* Paris, 1956.

————. *The Birth of Western Economy. Economic Aspects of the Dark Ages*, trans. E. M. WILKINSON. New York, 1961.

LEDAIN, B. *La Gâtine historique et monumentale.* 2nd edition. Parthenay, 1897.

————. *Dictionnaire topographique du département des Deux-Sèvres.* Poitiers, 1902.

MARCHEGAY, PAUL. *Notice sur les archevêques, anciens seigneurs de Parthenay.* (No date or place of publication.)

LE MARIGNIER, JEAN-FRANCOIS. "La dislocation du *Pagus* et le problème des *Consuetudines*, Xᵉ–XIᵉ siècles," *Mélanges d'histoire du moyen âge dédiés à la mémoire de Louis Halphen.* Paris, 1951.

MERLE, LOUIS. *La métairie et l'évolution agraire de la Gâtine Poitevine de la fin du moyen âge à la révolution.* École pratique des hautes études, VIᵉ section, les hommes et la terre, II. Paris, 1958.

PAINTER, SIDNEY. "Castellans of the Plain of Poitou in the eleventh and twelfth centuries," *Speculum* (1959), pp. 243–57.

————. "The lords of Lusignan in the eleventh and twelfth centuries." *Speculum* (1957), pp. 27–47.

PERRIN, CH.-E. *Recherches sur la seigneurie rurale en Lorraine d'après les plus anciens censiers, IXᵉ–XIIᵉ siècle.* Publications de la faculté des lettres de l'Université de Strasbourg, 71. Paris, 1935.

————. "Le servage en France et en Allemagne," *Relazioni del X Congresso Internazionale di Scienze Storiche*, III, *Storia del Medioevo.* Firenze, 1955.

PERROY, E. "Deux lignages chevaleresques en Forez au XIᵉ siècle," *Bulletin de la Diana*, 1956.

PORTEJOIE, PAULETTE. *Le régime des fiefs d'après la coutume de Poitou.* Poitiers, 1942.

RAISON, EDOUARD. *L'abbaye de l'Absie-en-Gâtine* (revised after the author's death by Marcel Garaud). Mémoires de la société des antiquaires de l'ouest, 1936.

REDET, LOUIS. *Dictionnaire topographique du département de la Vienne.* Paris, 1881.

RICHARD, ALFRED. *L'histoire des comtes de Poitou, 778–1204.* 2 vols. Paris, 1903.

RICHARD, JEAN. "Châteaux, châtelains, et vassaux en Bourgogne au XIᵉ et au XIIᵉ siècles," *Cahiers de civilisation médiévale*, 1960.

ROSTAING, CHARLES. *Les noms de Lieux.* Collection "Que sais-je?" Paris, 1958.

WERNER, K. F. "Untersuchungen zur Frühzeit des französichen Fürstentums," *Die Welt als Geschichte*, 1958–60.

INDEX

(Unless otherwise specified all place names mentioned are in the department of the Deux-Sèvres.)

A

l'Absie, monastery of: foundation of, 30–31; possessions in Gâtine, 31; urban purchasing for, 123; mentioned, 20, 35, 40, 66, 68, 72, 75, 76, 84, 85, 89, 99, 105 *n*, 107, 114, 115, 116, 117

l'Absie, village of, 22

Agriculture: elements of, 37–38; limitations on, 38; size of farms, 103; ownership of land, 103

Airvault, lords of, 66

Allod: incidence among nobility, 86; incidence among knights, 93; incidence among peasantry, 103

Allonne, Reginald, lord of, 74, 75, 76, 80–81, 83 *n*

Allonne, village of, 24

Anjou, counts of: feudal relationship with lord of Parthenay, 45, 46, 47, 48, 49, 53, 60, 62–63, 69; Fulk Nerra, 45, 129 *n*, 130, 131; Geoffrey Martel, 47, 48, 49; Geoffrey the Fair, 62–63; Geoffrey Grisgonelle, 129

Arbergamentum, 30

B

Bocage, 18, 21, 35, 39

Bois d'Allonne, priory of order of Grandmont, 123

Borderia; composition of, 32, 36–38; size of, 36, 103; origins of, 107

Bressuire, lords of, 28 *n*, 66, 72, 106, 116 *n*, 118

Burg: when founded, 26; structure of, 27; enclosures of, 27–28; founders of, 28; attraction of settlers, 28–29; inhabitants of, 121–24

Burgenses, 122–23

C

Cens, 86, 104

Chabot, Thibaut, lord of St. Hermine and Vouvant (Vendée), 66, 74

Champdeniers, castle of, 34, 58, 60, 72, 78, 90, 91 *n*

Champdeniers, lords of, 72, 74, 76, 83 *n*, 95 *n*

Chantemerle, lords of, 66, 90

Les Chatêlliers, Cistercian monastery of, 22, 30–31

La Chausserais, lords of, 72, 83 *n*, 95

Chemin des Chaussées, 22

Chiché, lords of, 72, 83 *n*, 98 *n*

Clientes, 120

Colonus, 102, 115

Commendize, 87, 110, 113

Complant, 30, 86, 104

Consuetudines, 108–9

Corvée, 107, 116

Custodia, 110

D

Decimarius, 117

Deforestation, 29–30

Domaine, 86

Dominium, 87 *n*, 108, 111

Dominus, 46, 72, 82, 95, 101

Droit de viage ou de retour, 51, 98–99

Droits d'usage, 105–6

E

Eleanor of Aquitaine, 63

138

THE JOHNS HOPKINS UNIVERSITY
STUDIES IN
HISTORICAL AND POLITICAL SCIENCE

*, *, *

EIGHTY-FIRST SERIES (1963)

1. The First Ottoman Constitutional Period
   By ROBERT DEVEREUX
2. Elbeuf During the Revolutionary Period:
   History and Social Structure
   By JEFFRY KAPLOW

*, *, *

THE JOHNS HOPKINS PRESS
BALTIMORE

THE JOHNS HOPKINS UNIVERSITY STUDIES IN HISTORICAL AND POLITICAL SCIENCE

A subscription for the regular annual series is $8.00. Single numbers may be purchased at special prices. A complete list of the series follows. All paperbound unless otherwise indicated.

ii